The James Wentworth Day
BOOK OF ESSEX
Photographs by Dennis Mansell

First published in 1979
Copyright James Wentworth Day

ISBN 0 905858 09 3

All rights reserved. No part of this book may be reproduced or transmitted in any form or by any means, electronic or mechanical, including photocopying, recording or by any information storage or retrieval system, without permission of the author.

Typesetting and design by
Art Anonymous,
Shortmead Street, Biggleswade, Beds.

Printed by S.G. Street and Co. Ltd.,
Church Street, Baldock, Herts.

The James Wentworth Day
BOOK of ESSEX

Photographs by Dennis Mansell

EGON PUBLISHERS LTD.,
19 BALDOCK ROAD, LETCHWORTH, HERTS.

To those who did the hard work — my wife Marion and my Private Secretary Mrs. Jean Gough — without whose aid and inspiration this book would not have been born.

Ingatestone,
Essex

Contents

Maldon – the key to Essex	6
Canewdon – where the Saxon throne was lost	14
Potton Island – haven of birds	20
The Chapel at Bradwell	24
River of rarities	32
Market day at Chelmsford	40
Colchester – jewel of East Anglia	46
The immortal Munnings	52
A railway to beat them all	58
Winged magic of the Essex shore	64
The Count of the Essex shore	68
The deer parks of Essex	76
Lord Petre's hounds	82
Audley End – the jewel of Essex	88
Mersea	96
The beauty of the Crouch	102
Essex – the dustbin of London	110
Canvey – island of history	116
The Wentworths of Essex	122

Maldon ~ the key to Essex

The ancient port of history and war, of raven-ships and smugglers, bull baiters, witches and wild-fowlers... the three-day battle of Danish triumph ... their great war camp at Danbury.

If I were to take an American by the hand and lead him to an English town which epitomised the history of England, I should take him to Maldon, the true capital of Essex.

The Romans defended it from their camp at Mersea Island and their great shore-castle of Othona at Bradwell-Juxta-Mare twin fortresses at the mouth of that noble river of beauty, the Blackwater. There, centuries later the Saxons built a fort, and the fate of half England was settled by axe and sword.

Up the river in 991 sailed Anlaf the Dane with ninety-three longships. Their banked oars thrashed the salt tide as the rise and fall of oars in Roman galleys and triremes had whitened the same seaway centuries before. The beaked ships grounded on the muddy foreshore of Northey Island. And there the Danes threw up a stockaded camp and marched ashore at the fall of the tide to meet the Saxon armies under Brithnoth, the Earldorman. This is no place to tell the tale of the battle which ended in the death of Brithnoth, the defeat of the Saxons and the triumph of the Danes who marched on through the streets of Maldon to set up their great camp at Danbury, whence they ruled the land with blood and sword.

It is all told in that splendid epic poem *The Song of the Battle of Maeldune*, 690 lines of ringing verse. There was much more of it, but the ancient manuscript, written soon after the battle had been lost, was partly burned in a fire at Dean's Yard, Westminster, in 1731.

Maldon has gathered light, life and colour from succeeding centuries.

There is the splendid library of Dr. Plume. There is Beeleigh Abbey, dozing in the sun by the side of the river where they first built it in 1225 or earlier. There is All Saints' Church, with a unique triangular tower and in the churchyard the unmarked grave of no less a man than the Rev. Lawrence Washington who died in 1652 never dreaming that his great-great-grandson, George Washington, was to become the founder of the United States. There is also the tomb of Edward Bright, who, when he died at the age of twenty-nine in 1750, measured seven feet round the belly, weighed forty-four stone and wore a waistcoat so vast that seven ordinary men could stand within it.

That long and many-coloured High Street which leads from the west end of the town, where the old coach road

Maldon in summer—a familiar sight, that is when the sun deigns to shower its blessings

from London comes in, and dips a mile further on nearby the Saxon church to the salt tides and the bright saltings, is a street of inns and houses built from Tudor times onwards. Elizabethan gables and doorways stand cheek by jowl with bland Georgian frontages and houses of Queen Anne grace. No man but a soulless hooligan "developer" would ruin the scene. Most of the streets deserve a protection order.

When Elizabeth I was Queen, Maldon was a great centre for drama. The feast of Corpus Christi was the high day for actors. We find that in 1453 the Corporation of this ancient Royal Borough paid two shillings and twopence to "the players of Lachydon; to the players of Sandon near Danbury, 20d; to the players of Wodeham-Ferrers, 20d; to the mystrallis of my lords Bourghchier (Bouchier) in here, mete and costs, 5s. 2d.". The Corporation very sensibly safeguarded its budget by lending costumes to "Colchester, Billericay, Baddow, Witham, Brentwood, Writtle and other places, and to the Earl of Sussex's players". Some of the theatre entries in the town clerk's book are bright little windows into bygone England.

Down by the river at Fullbridge there are flour mills and the oldest salt-works in Britain—they started making salt in Maldon a thousand years ago. A path runs by the river where you will see more swans than almost anywhere in England, to the old Abbey at Beeleigh that sanctified place of peace.

In the White Hart Inn yard, on December 30, 1784, they held a bull-baiting. The *Chelmsford Chronicle* of that day advertised it thus:

THIS IS TO GIVE NOTICE TO ALL GENTLEMEN
BULL-BAITERS

That there is a bull to be baited at Mr. Talladay's at the White Hart, Maldon, for a silver spoon of fourteen shillings value (the dog that runs best of three heats to be entitled to the spoon) on Wednesday, Old Christmas Day, the 5th day of January, and the second-best dog to be entitled to half-a-crown.

The bull to be at the stake at ten o'clock.

Dinner on the table at one o'clock.

It is easy to imagine that boisterous, bloodthirsty, dinner at the White Hart, but difficult to guess how the second-best dog spent his half-a-crown!

In 1890 they dug up a great oak post, three feet long and a foot square, in the Market Square. At first it was supposed to be the Martyr Stake at which they burned Stephen Knight, a butcher, on March 28, 1555, but it is much more likely to have been the post to which the Town Bull was chained on Sundays to be baited after church. The Chamberlain of the

A picturesque view of Beeleigh Abbey, the home of the Premonstratensian Canons in the thirteenth century. Now the home of Christina Foyle, of the famous bookshop in London

Looking from Northey Island, across to Heybridge at low tide

Town Council of 1732 records: "Paid to John Hance for a bull-rope and collar, £1 5s. 1d; paid to John Payn for keeping the bull-rope, £1 5s.".

Maldon was not only a nest of actors and bull-baiters, but, according to the evidence in a trial in December 1591, it harboured many witches who used "the wicked arts of withcraft, sorcerye and charminge, to the great offence and terror of manye people."

The belief is not yet dead. I have met many old men and women of Maldon and of the wide marsh country beyond who, up to twenty years ago, believed firmly in witchcraft. "Wise women", wizards and "cunning men" have been pointed out to me more than once, not only in Maldon itself but in that village with the enchanting name of Latchingdon-cum-Snoreham; at Canewdon, which once had a dozen witches, "six in silks and six in cotton"; on Wallasea Island where "old mother Redcap" terrified Alfred Martin, a farm labourer. He told me that he had seen her cross the creeks by moonlight at midnight on a wooden hurdle, without sails or oars.

Alfred Martin had been working at Devil's House Farm on Wallasea Island. This is his tale as he told it to me:

"Same as that owd Davvle's House. I know'd that well forty year agoo. An owd thatched place with a rare gret owd barn—suffin' lonely, I tell yer. I bided there a week. One night my mate found hisself hulled out o' bed an' down the stairs. He never know'd what done it. That owd davvle were strong as a hoss!

"Tew nights artewards he rowed over to Foulness Island across the crick. He come back late in the moonlight, bright as day that wore.

"'Alf', he say to me, 'what do you reckon I seed when I was a-rowin' acrost the crick? I seed that owd Mrs. Smith, owd Mother Redcap, from Foulness, comin' across the water on a wooden hurdle in the moonlight. She didn't hev no oars, but she travelled same as if she wore in a boat. She's the headdest witch about these parts. Yew look out, bor! She's on that island somewhere now.'

"An' yew believe me, sir, when we looked in the barn next mornin' there was that owd witch curled up in the straw like a cat. She come in the house, 'cause we had her son workin' along wi' us, an' I mind her well settin' by the fire, pellin' pertaters, nippin' her owd lips tergither, an' a-mumblin', 'Holly, Holly! Brolly, Brolly! Redcap! Bonny, Bonny!'

"Blast boy, she scat me. There was several witches them days, but that owd Mother Redcap was the headdest one o' the lot. I got out o' Davvle's House suffin' quicker arter that!"

In Latchingdon-cum-Snoreham there was the old woman who kept a nest of imps, horrible, snaky, naked little creatures, with semi-human faces, the size of mice, which she suckled under her arms. She could give you the "evil eye" and cast a spell.

Witches were feared, hated and appeased. If an old lady lived alone with a black cat, mumbled to herself, mixed strange potions in a saucepan over the fire, and smelt of brimstone, it was just as well to give her a pair of nice young rabbits when you had them, a couple of cabbages out of the cottage garden, or keep her in milk if you had a cow.

One poor old couple who lived at Fambridge were said to be witch and wizard. So the local inhabitants "swung" them both into the river Crouch, which was the surest way of proving whether they were guilty or not. The old man was nearly drowned, but was cleared of the charge. His wretched old wife was tied to a boat by a rope and floated. That proved she was a witch. Her life which had been a little hell, was thereafter a double hell.

Mr. Edward Knights, an Essex man born and bred, in his fascinating book *Essex Folk* (published in 1935) tells of another old witch named Hart who, he says, "lived in an old black weather-boarded cottage belonging to my great-grandfather at Latchingdon. The cottage was next to his own house and I have been told that my great-grandmother, in common with other country folk, used to have two or three baking days a week when supplies of bread and cakes were made, as in those days there were no bakers' vans running round. Witch Hart knew baking days, and generally presented herself at the door when my great-grandmother, being a kindly soul, used to give her a new loaf warm from the oven and a few cakes in the making of which she was an expert. One baking day she thought she would have a game with Witch Hart, and when the familiar footsteps were heard outside and a tap came at the door, she kept quiet and did not go to the door.

"But Witch Hart was not to be trifled with, and immediately set a spell to work with such muttering and mumbling and so effectively that my great-grandmother was suddenly taken ill. This so upset her husband that he at once took a generous supply of cakes and bread round to Witch Hart in an endeavour to conciliate her. These had the desired effect and the old hag was mollified, and on his return, he found my great-grandmother's condition improving. She continued to mend until she gained her normal health. After such an experience, Witch Hart never missed her bread and cakes until her death, when the cottage for a long time stood empty and was finally pulled down."

Hart seems to have been a common family name among the witch-sisterhood in the Dengie Hundred. Canewdon, where Canute landed his Viking forces to invade England, was famous for its witches. (Locals slyly hint that one or two are left today!). There were always six of them, three in silk and three in cotton. One was the parson's wife. One was the butcher's wife. When any one of them died, a stone fell off the church wall as a warning beforehand. Immediately another one was elected to the Sisterhood of Six. There was no lack of volunteers.

They were obviously muscular women because the legend is that they lowered one of the bells out of the church tower at Canewdon, launched it on the tide, and sailed up river!

Today, Maldon lives vividly with its past. There are still wildfowl in the river in their winter thousands and wild-

fowlers who go out in their frail punts in bitter weather. Maldon can still show the finest fleet of sailing barges on our coastal waters and the oldest sea salt works in Britain. Maldon Salt today is the fashionable fad in the great stores in London. Salt-crusted ships from the Baltic still sail up the river laden with Scandinavian timber. The town is a place of yachtsmen and yacht skippers, with every now and then a hopeful hero who hopes to sail his little boat round the world or across the Atlantic.

The beauty of the old town remains untarnished, its spirit invincible, its character unviolated. Beeleigh Abbey, that old house of monastic peace and gentle ghosts, sleeps upriver within its gardens and great reed beds where on a rare occasion you may see a salmon jump. There lives Christina Foyle whose name is a milestone in the literary world of today.

Down on the Hythe where that ancient little inn, The Jolly Sailor, sits comfortably at the foot of a steep hill crowned by a Saxon church, you will meet every sort of sailing man as well as those quiet heroes, the Maldon fishermen, a race unto themselves, masters of the sea. You gaze out down the river through a fresco of tall barge masts and sprits to the low shores and sparse trees of Northey Island, now, thank heaven, a bird sanctuary. There the Danish ships grounded and sent their sea wolves ashore to fight the Battle of Maldon, a keystone of English history. Too many towns in Essex have been spoiled by the cheapjack housing sprawls of the speculative builder. Maldon has kept its soul.

Sunset at Maldon—tranquillity by the seashore

Canewdon ~ where the Saxon throne was lost

Canute wins the throne of England on Ashingdon Hill... the great hand to hand fight... when all Essex was a place of blood and horror... Edric Streona the traitor who broke the Saxon army...

Following the bitter defeat of the English at the three day battle of Maldon in A.D. 991, England had groaned under the heavy tax of Danegeld. In the early autumn of 1016, however, the uneasy peace was at an end.

Terror gripped Essex from London to Shoeburyness, from the high downlands of Southend to the Roman city of Colchester. The fear of death stalked the land. Night after night the flames of burning villages lit the sky. Dead men and ravished women with their slain babies were food for wolves and ravens, eagles and the prowling wild cats of the Great Forest.

The enemy ships lay in the Thames, their sides shield-hung, their banked oars dipping in the flood tide, the banner of Odin floating from their mastheads, the ravens croaking their death song. The wild, blood-curdling war cry "Yuch Hay! Saa-a! Saa-a!" went down the wind. The Vikings were here.

Canute, the young King of Denmark, had come out of the eastern dawn with his proud longships, dipping their beaked prows to the silver shields of an autumn sea. It all happened over 960 years ago when practically the whole of Essex except the marshlands was covered by the Great Forest which stretched from London—hence Forest Gate—to the walled and towered Roman city of Colchester. For more than one hundred years, Essex, and indeed all the eastern shores of England, had lived in fear of constant Viking raids. The fork-bearded, golden-haired Danes in their leather jerkins, cross-gartered leggings and winged steel helms, stormed ashore with sword and battle axe.

Canute, son of Sweyne, King of Denmark, had sailed a year earlier to reconquer England. He had taken the Kingdom of Northumbria two years before that. He went back to Denmark, but returned with a mighty fleet of sail early in 1016. The Kent coast was plundered. A great Danish war camp was set up on Sheppey. Then he laid siege to London.

At the height of the siege, Ethelred the Unready died. His son, Edmund Ironside, the manly heir of a weakling king, determined to fight the Danes to the death. He raised an army in Wessex, defeated Canute's Vikings at the Battle of Selwood, and finally drove the Danes back to their war camp on the Isle of Sheppey. It seemed that the new English king

The old lock-up, dated 1775, by the entrance to the churchyard. Preserved inside are the village stocks of Canewdon

The church of St. Nicholas, Canewdon, with its massive tower of ragstone

was invincible. The long terror of the Danes might at last be at an end.

Canute set sail from the Medway and brought his ships and men around to the mouth of the River Crouch. There he landed on the muddy foreshore below the little hill of Canewdon (Canute's Don or Mount).

There Canute set up a stockaded camp, and, with the troops rested, fed and eager to avenge their many defeats by Ironside, he marched west above the marshes of the Crouch towards what is now Battlesbridge. It does not bear that name for nothing.

Edmund Ironside heard by swift runners that the Danes were in Essex on the south bank of the Crouch. With all speed, he marched his Saxon warriors through the dark trackways of the forest to meet the invaders.

The Anglo-Saxon Chronicle tells how: "When the King learned that the (Danish) Army were on the move, he assembled all the English nation, and went after them, and overtook them in Essex at the hill which is called Assandun, and there they boldly engaged together." This great battle took place on St. Luke's Day, October 18, 1016. It decided the fate of England for half a century.

We may assume that the Danes had already entrenched

themselves upon the high top of Ashingdon Hill where now stands the little church. The most reliable account of the battle is given by Florence of Worcester, who died in 1118. This is the tale:

"Edmund, flushed with the victory of his earlier encounters with Canute, was much the more confident commander; Canute led his troops by a slow march down to a level ground, while Edmund moved his forces forward much more rapidly in the order in which he had marshalled them, and giving a signal, fell suddenly upon the enemy. Both armies fought with desperation and many fell on either side."

It was mainly hand-to-hand fighting with long-sword, shield and battleaxe. The clash of sword on shield, the glint and murderous down-blow of battleaxe, the throaty war-cry of the Vikings and the screams and blood-gurgles of dying men, lit the autumn day with a splendid horror.

Edmund Ironside's Saxons, hard as nails, brave as lions, were winning that day. They had the Danes on the run. Many a sea-wolf would have been glad to have seen his longship waiting for him off shore at Canewdon.

Then suddenly, as the English army pressed forward and the Danes retreated, the right wing of Edmund Ironside's Saxons faltered and broke. Their commander, Edric Streona, who had been a favourite of the late King Ethelred and was an utterly treacherous, cunning fellow, had plotted earlier with Canute that he would desert Edmund Ironside at the crucial moment. He did so.

As the Danish army lurched backward in the imminence of defeat, the cry went up from Edric the Traitor: "Flet, Engles, flet Engles, ded is Edmond" ("Fly, English, fly English, Edmund is dead").

Edric brandished aloft on his sword-point the head of a soldier which he had cut off a moment before and shouted that it was the head of Edmund. Panic flew like plague through the Saxon army. Edric's own division fled headlong. The rest was chaos and slaughter.

Edmund, defeated, but defiant, arranged to divide the kingdom equally with Canute. Alas, he died of over-strain before the year was out and Canute became King of All England. He was a wise, practical monarch, generous and humane. He brought peace to the realm and was a devout Christian. Ashingdon was the birthplace of his power in Britain.

Today the church which overlooks the site of that historic battle stands on the top of a steep scarp 150 ft high over the marshes of the Rivers Crouch and Roach. Behind it, the inevitable suburban growth of villadom has largely

Ashingdon Church is dedicated to St. Andrew. The church was restored and rededicated in 1951. Below: The dedication panel

swamped the old village. But go to the church and you will get the spirit of the past in an atmosphere unspoiled.

The church was restored and rededicated in 1951 with monies raised in both England and Denmark. It had the singular honour of a visit from Prince and Princess Georg of Denmark. The scene is best described in the words of a charming little booklet by Anne Roper which I imagine one can still get at the church. She says:

"On a perfect English summer day, June 11, 1951, the Bishop of Chelmsford, with Prince and Princess Georg of Denmark, the Danish Ambassador, the Lord Lieutenant and his Deputies in their scarlet and gold uniforms, the Master of Corpus Christi, many distinguished guests, and the long procession of church dignatories, neighbouring clergy, cross-bearers, acolytes, and choir, white surplices billowing about cassocks of scarlet, purple, blue and black—the upstanding figure of the Danish Pastor lending a medieval air with his stiffly starched Lutheran ruff—all climbed the hill in solemn and joyous procession, singing the hymn *Lift High the Cross*, and then turned from the glorious June sunshine into the packed church for the great service of rededication and thanksgiving for the restoration of this ancient and historic heritage."

Interior of Ashingdon Church

Potton Island ~ haven of birds

A place of peace and beauty... the gleam of the sun on the dykes... redshank and curlew... heron and teal...

Potton Island, fifty years ago, was a place of peace and beauty, of birds and loneliness. I became shooting tenant of Potton Island in the 1920s for the princely rent of £25 a year. A thousand acre sweep of cattle-marsh with tidal creeks girdling it, and the sea wind in the torey-grass on its sea-walls. There were only two houses, one uninhabited, on the thousand acres, and only two inhabitants—the looker and his wife; three trees; a thousand sheep and a hundred and forty bullocks; two large half-brackish fleets, seven acres and four acres each; a sea of rough grass; a network of dykes; a smell of the sea; and a shifting population of fowl and waders, with a pair of marsh harriers, a few kestrels and short-eared owls, and an odd barn owl to police the lot.

So it came about that on a certain August morning I woke in a farm bedroom on the mainland with the dawn sun making frescoes on the wavy, whitewashed ceiling, a chorus of blackbirds in the garden plum trees, a hare on the lawn, and curlew and peewits crying on the mist-drowned pastures. London was very far away, and the world was young again.

A cold bath, a glowing skin, a great dish of bacon and eggs and tomatoes, and I was out on my way down a wild-rose bordered lane to the "hard" beyond the sea-wall where the boat lay.

My wife got aboard with the guns—I am one of those fortunate few whose wives are wildfowlers—while a handkerchief of a sail was run up and the boat put her nose into the flat, sun-patterned waters of the tidal river which washed two shores on the island. It was half an hour's sail up the river, up a creek, into another, all the while between saltings and cattle-marsh, with a world of birds and August colours to lighten the way. Herons fishing on the muds—you could see every feather through the glasses—curlew crying on the marsh, redshank piping up the channels, and now and then a skein of duck etched overhead against the perfect blue of an August morning sky.

An oyster-dredger lying in midstream, its tarred sides a beautiful and unearthly bronze in the dawn light; cows on the marsh wall, their cattle-smell strong on the air; straggling rooks above the sky-line; the smell of wood smoke and frying bacon from a half-awake boarded farm that lay like a stranded ship on the landward marshes; and over all the strong smell of the muds and of salt waters, the breath of sea-marshes, that indefinable something which, when you have known it, will dwell for ever in your blood.

Then the island farm came in sight, its chimneys and barn roof, with the top of one tall plum tree, sticking up above the sea-wall.

A shaggy, half-bred, half-wild cattle dog greeted us as we grounded on the "hard". His barks brought the looker, gum-booted, out of the barn, and we were told that the ducks would "likely still be in them dykes what run up ter the fleets.".

We set out from the farm with its wavy red-brown tumbledown outhouses—much the same as when van Cropenbrough and his Dutch reclaimers left it—through a sea of knee-deep silver, the mist swirling above the marsh like smoke. Peewits cried on the cattle-levels, and the island flats ran on farther than the eye could see in that mist-filled dawn.

I shall not soon forget that August morning. There is a peace on these sea-marsh isles which no other part of England knows—the peace of immense spaces; of a great wash of sea and sky; of mile on mile with neither house nor man nor road; the voice of a thousand sheep crying like an aerial undertone in the silence; the gleam of the sun on dykes and sea and tide-bared flat; the thin music of a little running wind creeping like a mouse through the long grass; the cry and wheel of curlew and shank against the dawn sky.

I suppose it was like any other day on any other sea-marsh, but one doubts if any day could be quite the same—the long, many-coloured sea of grass, bending like the break of rollers; the gleam and glint of blue water in dykes, straight-ruled across the marsh; the sign of tasselled reeds; the scent of grass pollen, and the sudden, astounding sight of four hundred curlew uprising in a cataclysm of wings from the green bosom of the marsh, the air alive with the harsh, grating "Kor-ew! Kor-ew!" of the old birds. Later, one found the small, fresh-water fleet where they had been feeding.

As we walked the long marsh-fields of lush grass with every now and then a gleaming, steel-blue dyke full of reeds to be jumped, we saw a sight which you will see only in England today on the remote marshes where time has stood still and the twentieth century halts at the distant railway.

You would have cried out in sheer protest had you been told to go down on your belly like a serpent and to crawl painfully, slowly, red in the face and red in the neck, baked by the sun, bruised by the earth, blinded by the streaming tokens of your own endeavour, progressing slowly, a yard at a time, the backs of your ears twin furnaces, until suddenly— a gleam of sky-blue water, a vision through the tall grasses of racing wavelets, crisping in the young wind. A vision, too, of a fleet of white gulls riding like schooners. A heron, blue-grey, statuesque, immobile among the shoreward reeds, and farther out a sheldrake, magnificent in chestnut and white, leading his family flotilla of six young and a wife. A group of mallard, their wives and young. A spring of teal, busy preening on a miniature mudbank. Redshank running like ballet dancers up the water's edge, and, on the far bank, that sight which you will not see, as I said, save in the forgotten corners of this land—four hundred curlew, feeding, sleeping, preening, with sentries alert to the flicker of a reed stem.

A sudden uprush of wings, a harsh, screaming cacophony of alarm. The vision of a cloud of birds uprising from the fleet. Squattering rushes on the water as the young duck bolted for the reeds. A hoarse "Fra-ank!, Fra-ank!" from the heron, who lifted like a blue-grey ghost from the reeds, and the world of birds that had been so peaceful, was about our ears in a frenzy of piping, screaming voices, of whistling wings.

One could stand up then, and the miracle was unfolded—the miracle of how that great, three-quarter-mile long lagoon of blue water could lie hidden in the heart of the marsh. It wound and writhed half across the island like a serpent, fifty yards wide where it ended at the distant sea-wall, and twenty yards from bank to bank where it forked off into two broad channels that went winding away on their own among the feeding sheep and the green marsh until they tailed off, one in a dyke and the other in a reed-grown splash that always holds duck in the fogs of early dawn.

Half a mile north of the Big Fleet lay another fleet, longer, but much narrower. The water was fresher, and so one often found more duck on it. Mercifully, too, it was easier to stalk. About it lay hummocks and mounds, with winding grassy gullies a yard deep, up which one could steal, rubber-booted, and so come suddenly upon the birds.

We did not shoot a lot of duck because I am no believer in big bags of wildfowl. They are beautiful to watch and therefore to be prized.

Potton remains down the long aisle of memory as an enchanted place of peace and birds, of sheep baa-ing on the lonely winds, and of timeless beauty. Long may it remain so.

The Chapel at Bradwell

History—description—Roman relics, etc.—the ghost in Walter Linnett's cottage.

The sea, wide and glittering, empty of smoke or sail. A sea into which the flat land merged imperceptibly till the verge of sea and land seemed one, a verge that melted from gold of wheat and green-blue of shining sea into the misty purple of sea-lavender. It ran on, that belt of purple between the gold and the blue, far to the south, far as the eye could see. And on it no man walked, no horned cattle moved. A moorland of the sea, such as Cornish knew and loved at Wells, far to the north where Norfolk meets the Icelandic swell.

A lost purple land enchanted by white wings of gulls, musical with the cry of curlew. And on the edge of this girdle of silver creek and purple salting, which married sea and land, stood a building tall and gaunt. A building of no architectural beauty, no grace of outline. Its walls, almost windowless, its high-pitched roof, gazed over the gold of cornfields and the glitter of sailless sea with austere uncompromise. Lonely as a lighthouse, deserted as a ruined castle, it offered neither the grace of the first nor the romance of the latter. Yet in it was enshrined half the history of Rome, the early whispers of the first English Christianity.

For the stones and bricks of which it is built came from that forgotten castrum of Othona, built foursquare, with its feet in the sea, when Diocletian was Emperor in Rome and the Count of the Saxon Shore was raised to high military honour and given charge of all those great, new Roman forts which guarded the English coasts from Portchester and Pevensey in the south, to Brancaster on the bleak shoulder of Norfolk. From Portsmouth Harbour to the Wash they threw a girdle of defiance round the coasts most open to Saxon pirates.

When you come to read the list of these nine forts of the Litus Saxonicum as it was drawn up about A.D. 428 you will find that this forgotten fort of Othona, on the lip of the Essex marshes, was first in dignity upon that list. The list is only shown in the Notitia Dignitatum, and the forts are shown as having been entrusted to three commanders, the Count of the Britains, the Duke of the Britains, and the Count of the Saxon Shore. And since that list is scarce and little known, and the Notitia Dignitatum is in itself a highly important document, I will give here the names of the nine known forts and their garrisons, since theirs is part of the earliest, dimmest-known history of our English shores. The garrisons and their forts were:—

St. Peter-on-the-Wall was probably built by St. Cedd in the seventh century It is the earliest Saxon building in Essex

25

1. The Commander of the Forensian band at Othona (Bradwell-juxta-Mare, Essex).
2. The Commander of the Tungrecanian foot-soldiers at Dubrae (Dover).
3. The Commander of the Turnacensian band at Lemanae (Lympne, Kent).
4. The Commander of the Dalmatian horse at Branodunum (Brancaster, Norfolk).
5. The Commander of the Stablesian horse at Gariannonum (Burgh Castle, Yarmouth).
6. The Tribune of the First Cohort of the Vetasii at Regulbium (Reculver, Kent).
7. The Commander of the Second Legion (Augusta) at Rutupiae (Richborough, Kent).
8. The Commander of the band of Explorators at Portus Adurni (Portchester, Hants.).
9. The Commander of the Abulcian Band at Anderida (Pevensey)

Those are the main known forts. But it is likely that there was another fort at Walton Castle, in Suffolk. It is now all swallowed up by the sea, so no man may trace it, that lost stronghold which also claims to be Portus Adurni. It, with the rest of the nine forts, was already in existence in A.D. 367. That much we know, for Ammianus Marcellinus mentions a comes maritimi tractus in that year.

It is possible indeed that these forts were built before the end of the third century. They followed the usual Roman plan of a square or oblong enclosure, surrounded by rampart and ditch with rounded corners. There were four gates, one on each side. Four main streets ran from the gates and met in the middle at the main barracks of the regiment. Officers' quarters, barracks, granaries, workshops, etc. occupied the remaining space within the walls. The ramparts were originally built of earth or turf, but gradually this was replaced by stone until by the beginning of the third century stone walls were universal. Gate towers were added later and followed by bastions or projecting towers all along the wall until in course of time each fort became a practically impregnable stronghold. Walls became high and stout. The gateways had narrow and crooked entrances and the walls were often thirty and forty feet high and from nine to fourteen feet thick. Such forts were garrisoned not only by regular foot-soldiers, but by cavalry and archers.

Pevensey and Portchester are probably the two best examples left in fair condition today.

Each fort was a combination of military and naval defence. Each stood on its own harbour and probably

The simple interior of the church at Bradwell

commanded its own little navy. Two, Richborough and Pevensey, actually stood on small islands, although today at both places and at Lympne, the sea has retired, leaving them high and dry a mile or more inland. It seems likely that these forts were occupied right up to the end of Roman rule in Britain, for there is a tile in the British Museum which shows that Pevensey was restored under Honorius.

I thought of this vanished Roman might of the gaunt, walled fort frowning seaward, of the little city and port which clustered without its wall, where now the tide flows and the mudflats gleam, of the eagles shining brassy in the sun and the trumpets shrilling brazen on the sea air, of all the hum and clatter of horse and foot and shipmen, as I came out of the tall wheat and stood in the sun looking at that gaunt, lonely building which rose thirteen centuries ago from the bricks and stones of the vanished Roman fort.

For all its humble loneliness, its earthen floor, and rush-seated chairs within, this old Chapel of Bradwell-juxta-Mare, this Capella del Val or St. Peter's-on-the-Wall, is the oldest and smallest "cathedral" in Britain today. For it was raised and consecrated by Bishop Cedd of the Eastern Saxons in A.D. 653, a year after St. Pancras, Canterbury. It is therefore the oldest existing church in Essex today. Bishop Cedd lived close to it, but whether on the site that is now Bradwell village, or hard by his own little "cathedral" no man knows.

You may still see, great courses of Roman brickwork two or three feet high running through the bushes east of the church. But they are all that is left of the old Othona. And even these few foundations had lain unknown, buried in the earth until in 1864, men working for a company called the Essex Estuary Company, which had been formed to reclaim parts of the saltings, dug down and uncovered these few remains. That good Essex squire, Mr. Oxley Parker, immediately commissioned Mr. Thomas Lewin to excavate the site and find out the extent of the fort and position of its ramparts. Then, and then only, was it clearly identified as having been a bastion fort under the Count of the Saxon Shore.

The little church or cathedral, as I have said, was built in A.D. 653 from the ruins of this ancient fort. Today it consists of a nave fifty five feet long and twenty six feet wide. The walls are two feet thick. Parts of the original three chancel arches, built of Roman tiles, can be seen in the east wall. The windows are original and the west one is almost perfect with a round arch of Roman tiles.

A big stone quoin at the north-west angle is obviously part of one of the gateways of the old Roman fort, for one can clearly see slots in the stone which were cut to take part

of a wooden doorway.

In Tudor and Stuart times the building was a beacon or lighthouse. Georgian smugglers used it to hide their contraband goods. In Victorian times it was a barn. Even within living memory cattle and sheep wandered in and out of it. Owls roosted in its rafters. The peregrines who quarter this lonely shore each winter like questing hounds whitened its roof-tree with their droppings.

Then, in June, 1920, having been given back to the Church by Mr. C. W. Parker of Down Hall, Bradwell, and wisely restored by Mr. Wykeham Chancellor, the little Saxon cathedral was re-opened to the worship of God.

It is today much as it was in Bishop Cedd's time. The walls are of bare stone. The chairs will seat a few worshippers.

Bradwell Chapel stands in almost complete isolation. The Othona fort built by the Romans as part of their coastal defences stood by the clump of trees on the right. It was partially destroyed by the sea

The Communion table is made from ancient oak beams left over from the roof of Chelmsford Cathedral.

All sorts of Roman relics have been found within a few yards of the church, coins ranging from Gallienus (260-268) to Arcadium (395-408), combs, needles, bracelets, and the beads of Roman women with the knives, weapons, tools and pottery of Roman soldiers, a steelyard and weights, fibulae and decorated pieces of bone, with bones of the wild boar, and piles of oyster shells from the table of the Commander of the Fortensian forces.

A tiny, four-roomed single storeyed cottage crouching at the foot of the Roman ruins on the *seaward* side of the sea wall. Built two hundred years ago to house a coastguard and his family, it was tenanted for most of the time by the Linnetts. Walter Linnett, the last to live there, looked like a Viking, lived by gun and net, was shy and silent, a strong man without fear. He shot more wild geese and duck than any other professional gunman on the coast. For forty years he gave me his friendship and from him I learned much. When he died his ten foot long punt gun, his old shoulder gun, his long single ten-bore and his punt came to me.

Then birdwatchers leased the cottage. They brought their hawks and falcons to this lonely place to fly them over the farmlands and the desolate saltings. And strange things happened. I described them thus in a book called *In Search of Ghosts* now long out of print.

Looking out from the sea from near St. Peter's Chapel

"On this night in July, 1964, Squeak, their Lakeland terrier, was in abject fear. He growled as he looked at the window and then looked at the two young birdwatchers asleep in the double-tiered wooden bunks against the wall. The growls woke Robert Knowles of Billericay, Essex, who works for his living in the Natural History Department of the British Museum. He looked towards his bedroom window and saw 'A man looking through. I could see him plainly. He had a big nose, dark eyes, a mournful expression and wore a seaman's jacket with a double row of buttons. I was just going to call out to him when he seemed to float through the window and, in an instant, was in the room not a yard from my face. He turned his back on me and was looking hard at Malcolm Chittleburgh who was asleep on the other bunk.

'Then I saw to my horror that there was no man at all from the waist downwards. Just a mist haze, a blur; Squeak, the terrier, was quivering with fright, crouching and growling. I was dead scared and called out to Malcolm.

'The figure immediately floated out of the window. There was enough light in the room for me to see the upper half of a man perfectly plainly and even to see the dog shaking with fright.

'Malcolm woke up instantly. When I told him what had happened, he was worried and most concerned because he told me he had experienced exactly the same sort of thing in September 1963 when John Willett, of Gidea Park, and another chap were staying in the cottage with him.

'They were all sitting by the fire in the living room when John Willett pointed to that same man peering through the window at them, not more than three or four feet away from their faces. He had the same sad look and he wore a seaman's dark pea-jacket with a couple of rows of big buttons on it. Malcolm had fully expected the man to knock at the door, but no knock came. So he got up and went to the door and looked out. The garden and the sea wall, the saltings and the greensward between the cottage and the old chapel and the gate at the end of the Roman Road were clear and white in the moonlight. There wasn't a soul in sight!

'Then all three went outside and searched the garden with a torch to make sure nobody was hiding in the shed, the old bakehouse, or in the wooden lavatory. There wasn't a sight of anything. They had all felt pretty scared. They kept the oil lamp burning in the cottage that night and went to bed with 12-bore shot-guns handy.'"

River of rarities

Almost anything may turn up—whales, swordfish, spoonbills, eagles, peregrine, the three rare birds and wild geese from Siberia.

"Same as rare birds", said Charlie, screwing up his eyes in the tobacco smoke. "I've sin a few in metime. Rum 'uns tew. Yew never know wots a-goin' to tarn up on this here owd river. Look at it now—ten or twelve moile long from this here basin down to the Main and tew or three moile wide. For ever o'mud. Tew big islands and gawd's amount o' little 'uns. Whoy, on a place like this here owd river anythin' can happen!

"I've sin a whale or tew in me toime. I've shot a salmon! I've tuk bass and grey mullet and sea-trout in me nets and I've sin a gret owd swordfish, nine fut six long, stuck up in a rill, not tew hundred yards from this here ship. Had a sword on him a yard an' a harf long. Lor! Wot a fish. I'd a liked to ha' let him loose up in Parliament to wake some on 'em up. He'd a-'gin a poke with that owd snout o' his'n! Yew rec'lect that owd swordfish, Mister Wentworth? Head masterpiece, warn't he?"

"Yes", says I. "The year before the war broke out. Stunk the place out for a week, what's more. But about these rare birds, Charlie . . ."

"Ha! I've sin a few in me toime. There was that owd flamingo wot owd Walt Linnett shot over on the Main. Rare gret owd bird, yard an' a harf high. Linnett was arter him fer a week afore he copt it. That kep' all on a-peekin' over the side o' Walt's punt every time he set up to it. That could see harf a moile. But Walt, he got on tew him one foggy mornin' and gie him 'peek' awright. Harf a pound o' shot—an' into a nice glass case he went!

"There was a eagle, big as a damn turkey, set on a post on the flats one mornin' and I've sin many a perrygrine hawk up this here owd river. They cum most autumns.

"Then there's them owd dutch owls (short eared owls). Allus a tidy few o' them on marshes. But git a year when there's a rare lot o' rats and rannies (field mice) about and them owd dutch owls'll cum over from Holland in droves. They fare tew know the grubs here a-waitin' fer 'em."

We were squatting on the bunks in the snug, lamplit cabin of the smack Hells Bells. Outside in the winter eve, the sea-wind of the Essex flats sang thinly in the rigging. The tide sucked and gurgled against the fore-foot. She was just beginning to lift off the mud, bump gently against the quay. Ashore the lights were going up in the pub windows. Fishermen, sea-booted, clumped by on the Hard. Charlie sucked at his pipe. His brown face, finely-cut, puckered. Salt winds and spume of half a century have etched the tale of a thousand dawn passages, down a hundred swatchways, in that face, which none but an Essex sailor could wear. It ought to be on the figurehead of a ship.

Salt water runs in Charlie's veins. They are all fishermen and gunners in that family. Why, was it not his old grand-dad, that night-prowling sinful free-trader, who dug up the bones of a hundred dead men from a cemetery on Foulness Island and sold the lot for bone-meal before his mates, the smugglers, scared him out of the graves! But that is another story.

Charlie blew out a cloud of stinking nigger-head. His mind was running back over forgotten shots under winter moons, trembling on half remembered visions of rare birds seen delicately in lifting mists of dawns on the lonely flats.

"I sin a spunebill one mornin'. Big as an owd frank-hern (heron). Lovely bird. White as snow. Cum from Holland. But there, Cor! Blast! Us fishin' chaps we see a helluva lot o'

birds wot we don't know nawthin' about. Same as we git a duck wot we don't know the name on we alluss call that a dunbird."

"Ha! Same as dunbirds", chipped in 'Chippy' Leavett. "I shot a duck one August the like o' wot I'd never seen a-fore. Gie that tew the Missus and towd her to hang that up and we'd hev it for Sunday dinner."

"'Wot is it?, she say. 'A dunbird, mate', I say. 'Don't you ask no more'.

"Cum Sunday there was a rare funny stink in the kitch-place. That owd duck had gone rotten. That stunk the house out.

"'That's a dunbird awright' says my owd mate. 'Thass done me a-cookin' on it. An' that's done yew out o' your dinner, mate! Yew can set down to bread an' cheese now'."

"Down on the Burnham river" I remarked, "they always call any duck that they don't know the name of a Russia duck. Remember when you shot those two garganey teal, Chippy?"

"Yis! Yis! There was foive on 'em flashed past me punt when I laid up in the Holes and I knocked out tew wi' one barrel. Thinks I, they're rum funny little ducks. I 'ont put 'em in the pan. I'll hull 'em in the pot for the owd dog. Then me married darter cum down from London fer the day wi' her chap. He's a Londoner—don't know a phizzent from a felfer (fieldfare). So I gie 'em the tew ducks, jist to see wot happen to 'em. Lor, they writ me that them tew little owd ducks tasted luvely. So I was the owd done bird that time!"

"How about them three rare birds wot Dick and Art shot on the Collins Bank las' week, Mister Wentworth?" suddenly asked Charlie. "Yew orter get on tew 'em. None of us never sin nawthin' like 'em on this here river a-fore. But look up, here cum the Guvnor. He'll tell ye."

Footsteps clumped on the deck above. Seaboots followed by blue naval trousers, topped by salt-stained battle-dress, the whole crowned by the grinning, weather-beaten countenance of Marster Leslie down the companion-way into the cabin. The owner was aboard, all six feet of him.

Son of a famous Harley Street surgeon, blown up at Dunkirk, riddled with bullets on Italian beaches, he fought all through the war as an Able Seaman and, long since, forswore the fleshpots and settled down as owner of the smack Hells Bells, registered as a fisherman-gunner. An old friend of rare diversity.

"Three rare birds! Never saw anything like them in my life" he exclaimed. "Most interesting. Dick and Arthur shot them last Wednesday. Here, take this down. You can write to

That vast expanse of water – Abberton Reservoir

Essex Countryside about them. Why, dammit, the biggest one weighed twenty-five pounds. Now put this down. Green heads, a splash of red over each eye, a green spine down the back of the neck, white waistcoats, the rest of the body mainly muddy grey and pink feet. What do you make of that?"

"A sunset" says I.

"Don't be so damn silly. I tell you they're unique. Old T . . . . . . has been crazy about them all the week. He's going to write to the Zoo about them. Says he last saw something like that in South America. He reckons they flew all the way across the Atlantic. Trouble is there's no-one on this river that's a real naturalist. Anything on earth turns up here and nothin ever gets properly recorded.

"Now, if that had happened in Norfolk, they'd have been identified in twenty-four hours and on show in Norwich Castle museum inside a month, with all the bigwigs among the bird experts taking photographs."

I saw a sudden vision of long letters in *Essex Countryside*, of a new name on the British bird list, of pundits from London taking trains to Essex, of sudden fame for two unlettered fowlers.

"Where's Dick and Arthur?" I asked.

"Over in the Jolly Sailor by now if I know their habits. Come on, let's go and see them."

We bundled up on deck in a frenzy of ornithological discovery, scrambled ashore and made a bee-line for the bland, comfortable, Georgian front of the waterside inn, with its yellow windows casting long, dancing, lamplit ghosts across the gurgling tide. A great cobgull barked high under the stars. I pushed upon the door and stepped into the boarded, lamplit, snug little bar. Fishermen and dogs, fowlers and winklers, oysterman and shepherds, clinked glasses and clacked dominoes. The coal fire, bright and blazing heated the place like an oven. Arthur, that Neanderthal man, with the frizzy hair, mahogany face, pushed-in nose and prognathous jaw, had half his face inside a pint pot; he grinned shyly sideways.

"What's this, I hear, Arthur, about you shooting the Zoo?"

He looked conspiratorial. "Don't do to say tew much", he whispered. "There's bin a rare clatter about it awriddy. That was this way. Me and me brother laid up in the smack in Death Crick. We allus lay there. Cum Wednesday mornin' arly, we shoved orf in the punt down to Collins Bank. Seed three gret birds set there, big as houses. Lor! They was a size. Never seed nawthin' like it. We set up to 'em, drored up to

sixty yard, let fly with the big gun, killed one and winged the other tew. They never even runned. They never even flacked. I hopped out on the mud, ups wi' me hand-gun and bowled 'em both over. They was all cullers o' the rainbow. Puts 'em in a bag, brings 'em back here, sold one to a man fer harf-a-quid and me brother and me et the other tew. Nex' morning the chap wot bought one cums back and says they're worth three quid apiece. Hed we got the other tew? Blast! We'd et 'em!"

"Yew was done birds awright then" remarked Charlie.

"Where are the feathers? I'll give you five bob for the feathers" I said eagerly.

"Bunt 'em! I bunt a bagfull on them" Arthur admitted mournfully. "Thought there'd be enquiration about 'em, p'raps tew much on't."

A moment of stricken silence. Through all minds ran the dreadful vision of epoch-making rarities lost forever to the records. The door opened to a gust of cold night wind. In stepped Alf and Cliff, my two blood-brethren on many a winter tide. Alf cocked a quizzical eye at me. Cliff sidled over.

"About these three rare birds, Cliff. Have you any idea . . . ?"

He cut me short.

"Rare birds. I can gie yew a rare bit 'o funny truth about 'em."

Arthur looked mildly apprehensive.

"We've jist cum up from the Island", Cliff remarked, savouring the effect of his words. "They bin on the telephone

A stretch of water at Abberton Reservoir

to the island farm from Stansgate abbey acrorst the river. About them three rare birds!" He paused dramatically. "Telephonin' all over the place. Police an' all!" Arthur swallowed his beer hurriedly, gave a quick look at the door.

"Wedgwood Benn's fancy tame geese—that's wot they were", Cliff went on. "Never flew a yard in their lives. Couldn't if they tried tew. They wus tew damn fat. Bur, lor, they managed to swim a moile acrorst that owd river, got up on the island beach and there they set. The looker runned down the beach, chucked his coat over one on 'em fell on him—and the b—— got away! They swum orf to the Collins Bank and there, I reckon, they set all night, pore things! Lorst theyselves a long way frum home. Pore owd things. Then the body snatchers got 'em!"

"Rare birds!"

A deathly silence brooded over all. The London pundits, the Zoo and *Essex Countryside* faded into the Land of Might Have Been.

The hard winter of 1978/79 with its jig-saw changes of weather, brought its own rare birds and bird mysteries. There was, for example, the mystery of the three hundred Brent Geese found dead, washed up on the lonely beaches of the Colne Point Nature Reserve near St. Osyth, on the Essex coast. The birds were fat and in good condition. They had clearly not starved to death. Nor had they been shot. The police were called in by the Essex Bird Watching Society and some of the bodies were sent for analysis to research stations at Cambridge University and elsewhere.

One theory was that the birds had been poisoned by local farmers who have suffered severe crop damage from the annual invasion by these small, but greedy geese. Brent are protected but several farmers I know have shot them in desperation. One man bagged about forty-eight in an hour using a light double 12 bore and No. 6 shot. The poison theory is, in my opinion, unlikely to be true for the simple reason that fields and crops were covered by several inches of snow—and who sprays snow with farm pesticides or any other poison.

My own theory is that the geese were probably poisoned by oil or other effluent from ships using the port of Harwich only a few miles up the coast from the spot where they were found dead. Meanwhile, from remote and lonely Foulness Island, the home of secret gunnery tests by the army, my friend Mr. Frank Burroughs who farms a large part of the island, says: "We had the usual influx of these geese a few months ago but when the snow came they cleared off. I don't object to a few hundred of them as their manure does the crops good but when they come in thousands as they did two years ago, the damage can be appalling."

His farm lies in the heart of what is the biggest winter gathering ground of these geese in Southern Europe. In that year of disaster another farming friend who shall remain nameless, lost £6800 of growing corn and grass in about a fortnight. The geese were in black clouds. The noise of them as they flew over my head was like the roar of great diesel engines in a railway terminus. I estimate that on one day another man and myself saw six thousand geese on the six hundred acres of the farm in question. This year, 1979, about two thousand are on the place, about one-third of the usual winter influx.

Another mystery is the reason for the remarkable number of the rarer sorts of geese which have recently visited the Essex coast. There was the lordly Snow Goose who arrived in stately beauty about three weeks ago and settled down on that great lake, Abberton Reservoir, not far from Colchester. There he is safe. Then there was the Red Breasted Goose which turned up not so long ago on lonely Potton Island which I rented in enchanted years long ago. It must have come from mid-Siberia westward across Scandinavia and the North Sea with one of the big packs of ordinary Brent Geese. The Red Breasted Goose is not only the rarest of those that visit us but it is the oldest wild goose to be the subject of a painting five thousand years old which I have seen at Maydoom in Egypt. This shy little goose which tames easily has unmistakeable colouring. It is black and white with red-brown throat and breast. It has a white patch between its eye and has a delicate black bill. It reached a lonely Essex island only to be shot down by a young farmer who mistook it for a Mallard.

The very rare Pacific Black Brant turned up and astounded all its beholders on Hamford Water, near Harwich, during this same hard winter. Normally this strikingly handsome black and white bird lives in mid-Siberia and in winter sometimes migrates to the Pacific and thence to the United States. This year's bird reversed the process and came West with a great pack of Brent Geese, as did the Snow Goose. That kills any hint that they might have been escapes from private collections. Another goose, not so rare but distinctly uncommon, is the Bean Goose, which is usually seen in very few countries. In 1979 there have been more than ever before. These winter skies are full of feathered mystery.

Market day at Chelmsford

Country Comedy—when the ferrets got loose... Langleys—that gem of a house "the best of the eighteenth century"... a church full of knights... some villages

Cattle mooing and bellowing at their own faces in shop windows, mounting the pavements, scaring the old women, dogs barking, rough men in long dirty raincoats herding the cattle back into the road again—that was the prelude to Chelmsford market day a few years ago when the beasts came into town on foot.

You remember the farmers in whipcord riding jackets, breeches, leggings and brown boots, rattling into town in high-wheeled gigs with high stepping trotters in the shafts or dog carts drawn by more sober beasts. Then there were the higglers and hen dealers in flat carts cluttered with crates of geese, ducks, hens, rabbits and ferrets—the lot drawn by hairy old ponies with philosophic faces. Flourish of long holly wood shafter driving whips, cracking their thongs, shouts and running feet. Horses neighing and whinnying to each other. Those were the sights and sounds that made country market day a merry day.

And by the time the farmers had filed into the Saracen's Head or the Golden Lion and eaten a belt-stretching "market ordinary" luncheon of roast beef, vegetables, Yorkshire pudding, country cheeses and celery for half-a-crown, and swallowed a few quarts of ale and a bottle of port, they were market-merry.

There were no fears of breathalysers when I was young. If you had a drop too much, you tied the reins to the dashboard of the trap, gave the old mare a friendly stub up the backside with the brass end of the whip and settled down to snooze. The old girl would find her own way home, by moonlight or starlight. It was all part of the drill. And she knew which pubs to stop at.

Those pleasant things no longer gladden the eye and the ear. Boots, breeches and leggings are out. And in any case, the modern farmer seldom rides a horse except out hunting. He jogs around the farm in a Land Rover or on a tractor. Some don't walk a mile a day. So trousers slipped into rubber boots are the gear. Some of the richer farmers and the potato tycoons wear expensive suits. Others stick to whipcord and tweeds.

Large saloon cars, Land Rovers and Range Rovers are run of the mill. The diddicoys—half gypsy, half God knows what, dark-eyed and dark skinned, smelly and cunning as rats—turn up in battered old vans loaded with scrap iron and second-

Not quite like the scene of an olden time market day, but the shopping precinct at Chelmsford is always busy

41

Chelmsford's cathedral is dedicated to St. Mary. An interesting church, in various ways, both inside and out

hand bicycles. Farmers hate them, but like fleas on a dog, they are always with us.

Cattle come to market not on foot but in single and double decker lorries which hold up to thirty beasts a piece. In Scotland, where the hill farmers still wear those warm and wonderful homespun tweeds, the sheep come south from the great Lairg sheep sales in huge three-decker lorries which hold up to sixty sheep each. It's meat on wheels and not on the hoof nowadays.

The cattle drovers are the same rough, long-coated, unshaven, noisy lot that their fathers were—agile as goats, strong as horses, and as loud-mouthed as Marxist shop stewards.

The higglers and hen dealers are still with us, sly as foxes, quick as ferrets, as independent as hedgehogs. They are a law unto themselves. Consider old "Noakey". He lives in a broken-down little old farm at the end of a steep lane on top of a hill. His old motor car won't start until it gets a free run half way down the hill. So Noakey loads it up with ducks, geese, rabbits, ferrets, and the rest, puts a wooden chock under a front wheel, mounts the seat, lets in the clutch—and yells to his boy "Knock her out, Bill". Away goes the wooden chock, the old car coughs, splutters, and charges downhill like a demented tank. It always works.

The exception was the other day when Noakey's old white mare came through a hole in the hedge just as the car was charging down. It hit her smack in the backside. Away she went like a Grand National runner. For fifty frantic yards that old horse would have won the Derby. Then she shot through an open gate and the car, snorting with frustrated blood lust, swooped out on the main road and headed for the market town.

Disaster came in the High Street. It coughed, spluttered, spurted steam and stopped dead. The sharp jerk caused pandemonium in the back. The ferret box lid flew open, the ferrets swarmed out and went for the rabbits and hens like avenging furies. Ducks quacked, geese honked, Noakey cursed and swore. Traffic piled up. Noakey was told in broad Essex where he came from, who his mother was, and where he was going to. The law appeared, notebook in hand.

" 'Ere, what's all this? You're holding up the traffic. Get a move on."

"Give us a bloody shove instead o' talkin'" said Noakey tersely. "Into the Saracen's yard. Them blasted ferrets are killing all my ducks and hens. Come on, guv, give us a shove."

The policeman bent down obediently, gave a mighty shove, and the car, uninsured, unlicensed and unroadworthy, rumbled and bumbled into the safety of the inn yard. The constable straightened himself and, knowing Noakey, said: "Don't let that happen again" and strode off. A certain God, peculiar to vagabonds watches over our Noakey.

Chelmsford, in spite of the London invasion, is still very much a country market town with a village spirit. Chelmsford has none of the beauty or history of Colchester or Maldon. The little Chelmer which noses its way through the town in a confidential manner has little charm. Chelmsford may be the county town but it has precious little architecturally to command attention. The modern rebuilding of much of the town destroyed a street of old shops and houses which was worth lingering in.

To offset its mediocrity, Chelmsford is surrounded by rich farmland and a scattering of villages which have kept

Fishing in the park at Chelmsford

their souls. Great and Little Waltham a few miles out of the town are part of the Langleys estate of some six thousand acres whose early eighteenth century manor house is one of the Jacobean gems of England. It was bought by Samuel Tufnell in 1711, enlarged and rebuilt with impeccable tase. The entrance lodge to the park is a tiny replica of the mansion itself, a little gem. It enchants the eye and rebukes the appalling bad taste of most modern architecture. The Tufnells still have it.

Other villages around Chelmsford worth seeing include Roxwell and Danbury. The latter was an old Danish camp which sits on a hill and gazes blandly over farmlands of the yeoman sort. Incidentally, it preserves a unique bevy—if that is the word—of knights carved in oak and another preserved in oil but not open to view.

Boreham has two classic manor houses—Boreham House, built in 1727 for Benjamin Hoare the banker, which gazes chastely down its long narrow lake, and the more ornate and historic New Hall, now a school, which incorporates part of an early mansion built by Henry VIII. A carved coat of arms in the chapel is of the same quality as you will find in the gateways of Christ's and St. John's College, Cambridge, and King's College Chapel.

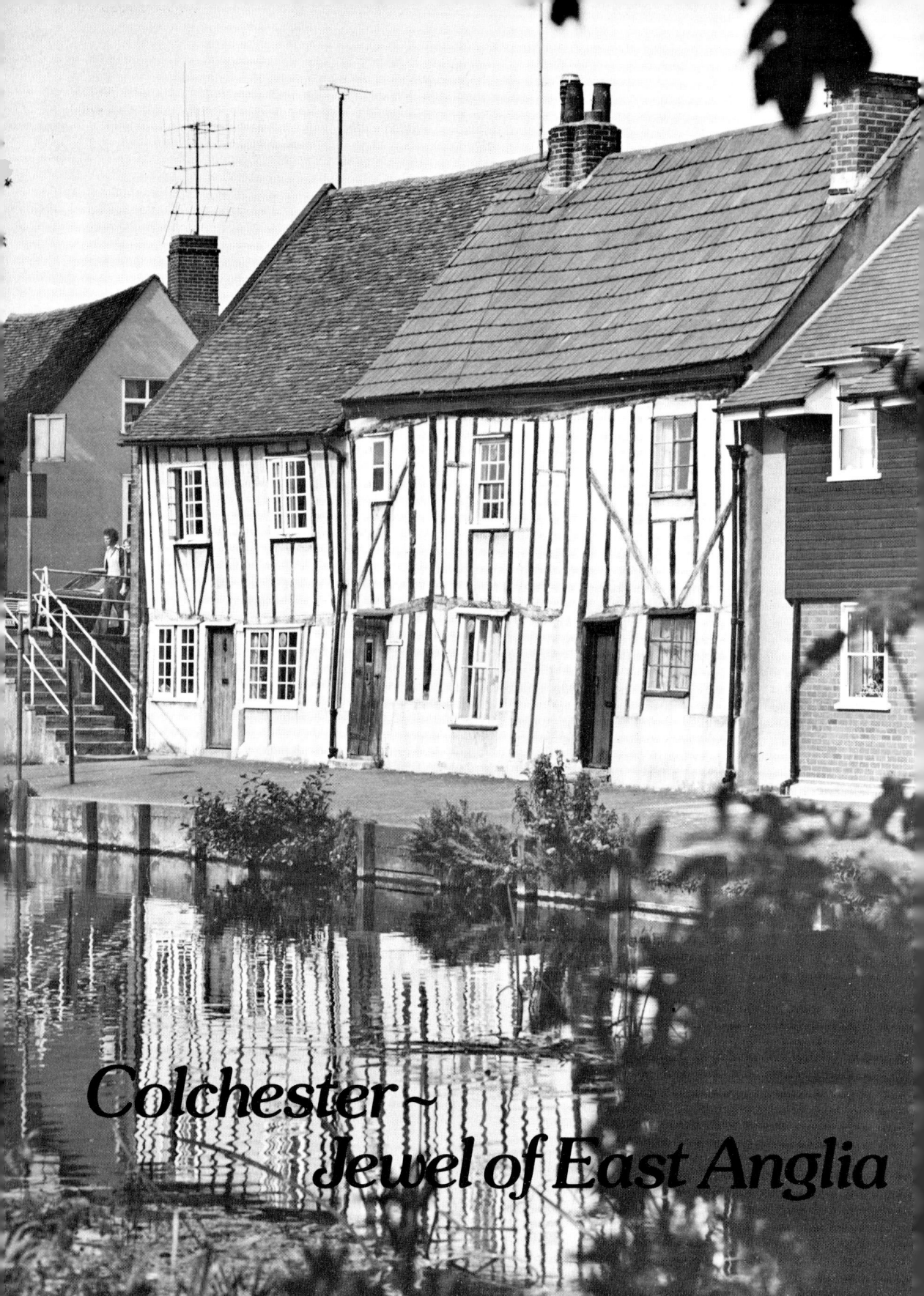

Colchester ~ Jewel of East Anglia

Where Boadicea humbled Rome... the oldest keep in England... the double murder in the moat ... town of churches and houses of grace—where plough and sail meet

"Where, if you have to live in a country town in the Eastern Counties, would you choose to dwell?" a friend, his eye on escape from London, asked. I gave him the answers categorically. First Cambridge, my native county town, shrine of ethereal beauty, and best of all universities. Secondly Norwich, the mother town of Norfolk, the breeding place of merchant princes and the nursery of a unique school of painters. Thirdly, Kings Lynn, with its thousand years of sea history, the water-gate to Norfolk and the Fens. Fourthly, an even tie between Ipswich and Bury St. Edmunds, if one had to live in Suffolk. Finally, but by no means last in my affection, Colchester.

This old town, puisant in Roman Britain, equally powerful under Normans, is today proud and lovely, the jewel of time, smirched a little by the bleak materialism of modern architecture, but unique. Where else can you walk down the High Street, the sea sharp on the wind, the largest Norman castle keep in Europe looming ahead, a glimpse of Dutch houses down a side street, a vision of Georgian and Queen Anne grace framing the view ahead, with Georgian and Tudor hostelries beckoning you away from the challenging charms of a little pub built on top of the postern gate of one of the greatest Roman fortresses in Britain? Another side street opens to a bright horizon of barley fields and wheat stubble.

This country town has been successively a Roman fortified city sacked bloodily by Boadicea, a Norman fortress which Cromwell knocked about, and always a port of note whence ships sail and merchandise comes in. In short, a microcosm of English history. A town with the patina of age, the robust bustle of country trades and sturdy crafts. Strong sea-winds beat about its roofs. Wide marshland downs enchant the eye. Deep woodland and gorse-gold heaths where you may ride a horse all day and scarcely touch a main road. That is Colchester. The town of my delight. The town at whose annual Oyster Feast you may swallow oysters by the dozen with gin and gingerbread and ancient salt-water rites to glorify the swallowing.

Colchester has grace, beauty, dignity, history, commercial life, country sturdiness and alas, in its High Street, some modernistic horrors.

Colchester is a city with a soul. A place of civic pride which has married industry and new housing with such

Cottages beside the River Colne at Colchester

47

William the Conqueror used stone from the original fort to build the keep at Colchester, which is England's oldest recorded town. The 100ft. keep is the largest in Britain. Its museum contains a magnificent collection of Roman relics

precious jewels as "the Dutch Quarter" of Stockwell Street where half-timbered houses with over-sailing upper stories lean across the narrow ways in ancient friendship. The Castle Keep, built by William the Conquerer, is the largest in Europe and stands within the perimeter of the old Roman Forum. It is now a museum with one of the finest collections of Roman remains in this country and a great many other good things. Girdled by green moats and grassy ramparts, it sits, a grey and rose jewel amid bright gardens. In one of those gardens stands Holly Trees, a red-brick Georgian mansion, another museum, with an entrancing collection of period pieces.

Across the road an old church has been "unfrocked" and now houses a natural history museum of the more intelligent sort. Apart from stuffed birds and animals and odd monsters from the Essex seas, it is a home for wounded creatures of the woods, fields and marshes, which are there nursed back to life and strength. You might walk in and find the Curator, tending a motherless fox-cub, a couple of oiled-up seabirds, a badger released from a trap or a wild duck with a broken wing. The door is open to them all.

Colchester, like Norwich, can claim to be a "fine city". It has not only the remains of a splendid castle but a magnificent Abbey gatehouse, fine old churches and the remains of city walls which are notable by any standard. The Royal Commission lists the remains of ninety-two Roman buildings within the city walls and fifteen outside them. The remains of more than fifty mosaic and tessellated Roman pavements have been found. Some are now in the Castle museum. The architectural rival of the Castle, though not on so grand a scale, is the ruin of St. Botolph's, one of the great monastic

An impressive fragment of an early Norman church – St Botolph's Priory. It was founded in the late eleventh century as the first British house of the Augustinian Canons

Looking through the Balkerne Gate at the Mercury Theatre and 'Jumbo', the name given to the red brick water tower which dominates one end of the High Street, Colchester

churches of the eleventh and twelfth centuries. No less than seven medieval parish churches lie within the city walls.

The town is dominated, oddly enough, not by the Castle Keep, but by a monstrously massive Water Tower put up in 1882, known far and wide as "Jumbo", the tower of the Town Hall erected in 1898 and the spires of St. Nicholas in 1875, the Congregational Church of 1884 and the "new" square tower of St. Botolph's of 1838—an assortment of Victorian buildings which hardly prepares one for the tremendous wealth of medieval and Georgain houses and the rich fields of Roman remains.

The British King Cunebelin who created the first Colchester, called it Camulodunum, after the Celtic war-god, Camulos. It lay south of the river, up the hillside. On the west it was protected by huge ramparts which cut off the peninsula between the Colne river and the Roman river, and long stretches of these remain. The inhabitants of Camulodunum traded with the Continent and a tumulus in Lexdon Park opened in 1924 revealed a wonderful treasure of bronzes, armour and ceremonial furniture, gold tissue and silver ornaments now in the Castle Museum.

The Roman colonia, established in A.D. 49-50, owned a vast acreage of land and its great temple of Claudium dominated the countryside. In A.D. 60 Boadicea and her Iceni sacked Camulodunum, massacring the inhabitants and destroying the temple.

The town later became an important Roman manufacturing centre, fortified with walls which stand today. The private houses were solidly built, centrally heated and enriched with tessellated pavements. Public buildings included several large temples, and two theatres. The main streets of the Roman town have become the main streets of modern Colchester, except that the High Street once ran through to the Balkerne Gate in the west walls, while today it stops at the line of North Hill and Head Street.

At the time of the Norman Conquest, Colchester was populous, with about seven churches. From the thirteenth century onwards Colchester was a great cloth-making town, famous for "bays" or baize. It remains a considerable cloth-making centre today.

In the Civil War a Royalist force held the town against the Parliamentary army for eleven weeks in the summer of 1648. Cromwell's cannon did a lot of damage, but starvation defeated the gallant defenders. Their two heroic leaders, Sir Charles Lucas and Sir George Lisle were shot—I prefer the word murdered—by General Fairfax, the Parliamentary leader, who had neither the soldierly qualities nor the gentlemanly instinct to treat brave opponents with chivalry. From 1840 onwards, Colchester, after being down in the dumps, doubled its population by the end of the century, built the elaborate Town Hall in 1889-1902 and went on the flourish like the green bay tree. It still does.

It is still a brisk country town with its roots in the farms, woods, heaths and marshes which surround it. Where else could you do as I have done many a time—ride a strapping great sixteen-hand hunter up the High Street on a busy Saturday, turn in under the timbered archway of that good old Tudor hostelry, the Red Lion, chuck the reins to the doorman, the immortal Albert who looked like an ostler in a waistcoat and loved horses, and stump, booted and spurred and muddied, into a glorious beamed and raftered Grill Room where a steak, sizzling from its charcoal bed, and a bottle of Chateau Latour were the keys to heaven. And not an eyebrow lifted. They take that sort of thing for granted in Colchester. Just part of the everyday scene with the sea captains up from their ships at Hythe; the farmers in from their moated farmhouses; the oyster fishers from Mersea Island; the barge skippers from Brightlingsea and Wivenhoe; the artists from Constable's Dedham Vale where Munnings later immortalised the river, the bright barley stubble and the woods of lucent green.

These scenes of quiet and spacious beauty encircle Colchester. Ten miles away to the east over the bridge that spans the little Roman River, through the woods of Donyland and Fridaywood you come to the Peldon Rose, an inn five hundred years old sitting at the crossroads where the Romans threw the great causeway called the Strood across the saltings, the mud-flats and the salt water channel into the Mersea Island. The Strood still goes under water at high tide.

Mersea is still an island, five miles long, a mile wide, with its Old City of tiny clapboarded cottages and its manor farmhouses out in the fields.

At the Peldon Rose, the smugglers hid their barrels in the pond by the inn. The Strood is haunted by the clanking ghost of a Roman Centurion in armour. They say that two Viking chieftains fought to the death for a Saxon maid on Barrow Hill. And in Copford Church, the other side of Colchester, you can still see, nailed to the door, the last brown, shrivelled remnant of the human skin of a Viking raider who was flayed alive.

Colchester and its countryside have as many facets of charm, beauty and history as a diamond ring has flashes of light. This old Roman city, still vivid and vibrant, is the central jewel.

The Balkerne Gate, Colchester

The immortal Munnings

The Essex Painter who made art history . . . Apostle of the horse . . . an era of enduring beauty

We were driving back from Newmarket in the deep peace of a summer evening in 1959 when, at Stratford St. Mary I said suddenly: "We are in the Munnings' country. He lives only a mile or two off the road at Dedham. I'll telephone him." So we stopped at the Swan and I rang the man, who more than any other painter stirred the art world to its depth.

"Alfred, I'm with my spouse only a mile or two from you. May we drop in for a few minutes."

A sad, deep voice growled: "I'm not fit to see a dog. I've done with this world."

"Nonsense," I said, "You've got another book in you yet. Your three decker memoirs are absolutely classic. Time you wrote another one. Search your memory. It will come to you."

"Only one thing will come to me—the grave. You can write my epitaph." He put down the telephone. Six weeks later he was dead. His ashes lie in St. Paul's Cathedral. His memorial tablet next to that of John Constable in the crypt of St. Paul's bears these words by the Poet Laureate:

O friend, how very lovely are the things,
The English things, you helped us to perceive.

I counted Alfred Munnings, President of the Royal Academy, and the greatest outdoor painter of this century, as a beloved friend. As a painter he was unique. As a man he had as many moods as a woman. His paintings of horses of all sorts from gypsy nags to Derby winners are without rival. Never since the days of Stubbs, Sartorius, Ben Marshall, Alkens, Herring and Ferneley, has the horse been so glorified on canvas. The genius of Munnings lay in something which most of the other great horse painters lacked. Fidelity to the moods and movements of the horse. Too many of the great horse artists painted their horses like statues or with all four feet off the ground at once, something which no living horse has done or could do. Munnings, who has studied the anatomy of the horse with infinite care, gave the animal new and lasting life. His horse portraits were the sensation of his day. They remain his lasting monument today. That was why kings, princes, dukes and mere millionaires bought them as jewels of beauty.

No man was a truer East Anglian. His father was the miller of Mendham Mill. His grandfather farmed Scotland Place Farm, of about seven hundred acres near Stoke-by-Nayland in the Essex/Suffolk border country. Before his

Castle House, Dedham, the home of the late Sir Alfred Munnings

father went to Mendham he had Shonk's Mill, near Ongar, in Essex. His grandmother was a ringer of Walsham Hall. Four hundred years before that the Munnings, or De Munnines of Norman descent, farmed at Nedging. So he had a root in every Eastern county. Finally he came back to Essex and lived at Castle House, Dedham, old and gracious amid green meadows, with the shine and shimmer of the River Stour in the foreground. There, the man who had learned to paint in Norwich, where his early works fetched a few pounds only, rose to the pinnacle of his fame. He saw his pictures fetch tens of thousands of pounds. Today, the collection of his works in the house at Dedham is worth about half a million.

As a man he could be a firm friend and a bitter foe. He loathed pretence and anarchy in art. He attacked and ridiculed the vendors of modern so-called art, the futurists, cubists, rank anarchists and creators of abstract nothingness who caught the magpie minds of the half-baked in a tidal wave of ugliness for too long. His private feud with Sir John Rothenstein, Director of the Tate Gallery, was a duel of sheer eighteenth century malevolence.

Yet Munnings could be the essence of tenderness, the quintessence of Victorian sentimentality. He wrote with the pen of a poet. He painted like a dream. I remember these

Mellowed buildings of character in the High Street, Dedham

few paragraphs in his diary, describing the morning song of larks over those empty, rolling downs of North West Essex, and high above the Devil's Ditch on Newmarket Heath:

"Ten or fifteen years ago I sat here hearing the tune of the wind blowing through tall, seeding grasses, increasing and dying away like . . . 'The horns of Elfland faintly blowing'. . .

"But how can one describe the incessant music of the skylarks? Many are in the air at once, ascending or descending, for there is no cessation of all this music, which goes on and on, and one wonders from how far off the faintest song may reach. To look up and search for a sign of the birds is useless, not one is in sight.

"It is a hot day of heavy broken cloud, with the wind in the south. Only the commonly used word 'balmy' can give expression to my feelings. It brings to mind an old sentimental song, set to a waltz refrain:

" '*Oh, winds that blow from the south*
Sighing to soft and low . . .'
but soon aeroplanes begin to dispel, disturb and shatter the calm."

I have outstanding memories of him. First a dinner at Castle House, Dedham, when he announced:

"Tonight we are drinking nectar—the drink of the Gods. Walter Sichel is the Gods' salesman on earth!" And out came the bottles of that superb Rhine wine Niersteiner Hipping Sylvaner Beerenauslese, a wine which as the Prince Regent once said of that other great wine Chateau Palmer, is "as soft as the Holy Palmer's kiss".

When dinner ended and the vintage port went round, Alfred rose from his chair, stepped into the centre of the dining table and without upsetting a glass or causing a decanter to quiver, recited his own unforgettable "Ballad of Anthony Bell" which John Masefield, Poet Laureate, once said was one of the greatest hunting poems in the English language. I have it now in Munnings' own handwriting, ten pages of it. He could declaim like a poet and sing like a cock linnet.

The second picture was of Alfred with his old friend Fred Bowcher who had a good deal of money, owned a number of good horses including Cryptical who won the National Hunt Steeplechase in 1928 and was a member of the Jockey Club. He dressed like a scarecrow. A policeman once tried to bar his entry to the Members' Stand at Newmarket. He lived at Langham on the Essex border. A bachelor, he was looked after by devoted old sisters. The old house was furnished mainly with "standing armies of wine bottles of every description" including jeroboams of Champagne, great crates of

There are plenty of places away from the crowds all along the Essex coast, especially in winter. This stretch of the River Stour is in "Constable Country", between Manningtree and Flatford

Sichel's Berncastlers and hocks, brandy, Chartreuse, Benedictine, but not spirits. The bottles stood on the floor because the sideboard could take no more. Cigar boxes were piled on top of the piano till they almost reached the ceiling. Yet his old maiden cousin, Annie, played Mendelssohn and Beethoven on it on Sunday afternoons. The sofa was piled with racing calendars, Sporting Lifes, horse sheets, weight cloths and more boxes of cigars. What room was left was taken up by hunting boots, fishing waders, rods, guns, and rotting apples which had been put down and never picked up and eaten. An old tortoiseshell cat never stopped having kittens. If she wasn't in the easy chair the black and white cat was. When both were absent the sandy cat took over. His golden retriever tolerated the lot.

"There", said Alfred, pointing to Bowcher, in his disreputable clothes and an old straw hat with a hole in it, "is a real Englishman—but a bit of an eccentric." Never has a pot called a kettle so black before.

There was the day in his Chelsea studio when the man who at his worst could deride, lampoon, curse and excoriate the modern murderers of art—Chagall, Braque and Picasso and make Sir John Rothenstein squirm, turned to me with a hurt look and said, pushing a newspaper into my hands: "Look at that. One of your damned newspaper pals, an art critic, not yet out of his nappies, calls me 'That old man of Newmarket who can only paint horses.' Hasn't the damned fool ever seen my White Canoe with all its summer river peace and not a horse in sight? Or Flatford Mill in Winter with nothing but ice and snow and stark trees or The Full River with the wind in the willows with not a filly in sight."

He glared at me, genuinely wounded.

"Alfred", I said gently, "every animal has its parasites. So has Fleet Street. These callow little half-baked art critics who have never painted a picture in their lives and can't earn a living in any other sphere of journalism, come out of their holes in Chelsea like ferrets, hiss and bolt back." The simile pleased him.

"Ferrets! Yes, ferrets! But I'm nobody's damned rabbit!"

There was that other day at luncheon in the Athenaeum in Pall Mall when the Club dining room was full of bishops, judges and professors. I told Alfred that I wanted him to support my crusade against the proposed Bradwell Atom Power Station at the mouth of the Essex Blackwater. It would, I said, ruin a noble river and drain millions of tons of water from his own beloved river, the Suffolk Stour.

"Water", he suddenly roared. "Water—I'll tell you why we're short of water. Every time an old woman piddles half a

pint, she pulls the chain and away goes a gallon. That is where the water goes. When I was a boy, we used a bucket, chucked it on the garden and grew better lettuces."

The luncheon chatter died. There was a shocked silence of reproof. Then a voice said clearly:

"O God, there's that ostler fellow at it again!"

The name stuck. Alfred looked like an ostler and sometimes wore the sort of waistcoat that ostlers wear. Later he had to go before the committee and apologise for his conduct after he had pinched the shapely behind of an Irish waitress and told her she was "a damned good paintable girl".

Those were some of the moods of the man who was happiest travelling the lanes of Essex and the heaths of Norfolk in his gypsy caravan with his friend Drake who was sunburned, with queer blue eyes, and dressed in the gypsy way with a black silk neckerchief, a long brass-bound whip in his hand. At his heels a Norfolk lurcher, which snapped up hares and pheasants and brought them like a ghost to its master.

And so into the sunset with the rising moon, the scent of dog-roses, honeysuckle, the smell of road dust, the sounds of horses' feet and the Norfolk voice of Shrimp telling him of his last appearance before the magistrates. And now the sun has set, the memories remain. The flame of his genius will light the English scene for ever.

Paddling their own canoe in the placid River Stour at Dedham

The Crab and Winkle... Kelvedon to Tollesbury in a cloud of steam... the village gossip forum... cows on the line... and a pause for a partridge shoot... the last of Tollesbury Pier

Do you remember the Crab and Winkle Railway, pride of East Essex for nearly half a century? There was no railway quite like it. Until a few years ago the odd corners of Britain had their own odd little railways. Each had its local nickname.

I mourn the Goose and Dicky which served the swampy Broadland villages from Yarmouth. I lament the Crab and Winkle. Nostalgically I remember the Land 'em, Cheat 'em and Dump 'em—London, Chatham and Dover. I salute the dead, including the Clare Crawler of mid-Suffolk. Alone, the Bluebell in the South and the Eskdale in the North—saved by the love of such oddities as you and me—survive.

They were fun, our little country railways. The last breath of rural Victoriana. The authentic puff-puffs of childhood. The pride of the villages. High adventure to old ladies. Almost a hint of sin to the old bearded gaffer when he put on his Sunday best, complete with age-green bowler, and boarded the train: "Ter goo and visit me darter what lives furrin." She was somewhere up in "the Sheers", that ungodly hinterland peopled by black-advised men with malignant minds!

Then there was that immortal tale of the opening of the Great Eastern Railway in grandad's time. Somewhere along the line there is a tunnel and when the line was opened in the tranquil days of the last century, Jimma bor and Billa bor discussed the momentous event in the inn that night.

"Ha' you sin that li'l owd railrood, Jimma bor?".

"Noo, thet Ah hee'ant. Ha' yu?".

"Yis, bor. Thet run roight at the bottom o' my master's tharty acre. Sharpas yar owd clock goo ten in the mornin'. An' du that travel! Thear ain't a hoss in the parish what could ketch it—nor yit a long-dog. Do yu goo ond see that, Jimma bor."

"That oi will, owd mate."

Sharp at ten the next morning Jimma bor, his missus and the kids sat like a row of rooks on the five-barred gate above the railway tunnel. On the stroke of the hour the train trundled by in a blast of steam and sparks, gave a piercing whistle and plunged into the dark tunnel, a dragon's tail of sulphuric smoke waving behind it.

That night in the four-ale bar came the sequel.

"Ded yu see that li'l owd railrood, Jimma bor?".

Easterford Mill, Kelvedon

"See ut! That oi did. Travel, bor! Oi niver seed nawthin' travel that fast in arl moi days. There warn't a hoss at Newmarket what could ha' ketched it. That come a-roarin' an' a-hissin' an' a-flamin' up the valley loike the Davvle hisself. But blast, bor! That ain't that that travel so fast. That ain't that that make so much row. Thass a double-cunnin b——, that is! That no sooner sets that's eyes on me an' the missus an' the kids than that shruk like a hullet (owl) an' hopped down a hole like a rabbit!".

What is your favourite childhood memory of such enchanting railways? My mind goes back to a September morn. That Imperial Emmett of all trains, the Crab and Winkle, blundering along through the broad bright Essex fields. Past cottage gardens and apple trees, red with fruit. Behind us, that old, old town of Kelvedon where Tudor jostles with Queen Anne in a bland gallimaufrey of careless beauty. Ahead lay the glimmering sea, the green and silent marshes.

They had a cow-catcher on that train for you never knew when you might have to shovel a bullock out of the way. You could stop the train where you wanted it to stop. In the

The tranquility of an English village. Feering, Essex

middle of a field for instance. I stopped it at night by waving a torch from a field gate.

The carriages were long, with seats up each side, so that two rows of villagers sat facing each other. And there was an observation platform. You could stand at the end of the train and survey cattle and pigs, the ploughman and his team, the wildfowler prowling up the dike-side or the fishing fleet standing out to sea in a clutter of red sails far down the shining creek.

On that September morn, I stood, gun in hand, on the observation platform. The guard had warned me that a covey of partridges took their morning dust-bath beside the track. Sure enough, up they got in a whirr of wings. And a double shot cut a brace over, as neat as cricket balls. We stopped the train. Engine driver, guard and gunner searched the rough grass. The birds were found. The train re-started. Off we went. And two railwaymen had game for their Sunday dinner.

In those days I used to travel each weekend to Tollesbury by the Crab and Winkle to stay with the late Count de la Chapelle at Heron Lodge, his shooting box overlooking the marshes of the Blackwater Estuary. From the bedroom windows, one could see the pier stretching far out into the shining estuary.

Almost at the foot of the garden ran the railway line down to the Pier Station—a railway coach and a small brick building. That was about the sum total of most of the "station buildings" on the nine and a half miles of track. Everything was informal, individual and charming. The engine was a shining museum-antediluvian. Everyone knew each other. A great place for gossip and exchange of village news. Some of the coaches had an outside railed platform with a roof. One could stand there, contemplate the sunlit beauty of unspoiled Essex and wave to friends that worked in the fields.

At each crossing, the guard got down, opened the gates while the engine stood puffing and spluttering, and let it through. Then he closed the gates, sauntered back to the train, climbed aboard and off we went. There was no jet-age nonsense about the Crab and Winkle.

The line was first proposed by Sir William Abdy, Bart., who owned Barn Hall at Salcott and about 2200 acres of land. He gave five acres for the line. Others sponsored, including Mr. Alex B. McMullen of Guisnes Court, Tollesbury, and Mr. Arthur Wilkin of Tiptree gave twenty-five of the fifty-three acres needed. The Treasury put up £16,000 as a free grant. Other "under-takers" of the line were Dr. J. H. Salter

The pond at Tiptree makes an attractive feature in the centre of the village

of Tolleshunt d'Arcy, one of the greatest characters Essex has ever known, and Mr. James N. Paxman. Sir William Abdy gave £200 and Mr. McMullen £100 to a fund of £650 set up to buy the remainder of the land. Stations or sidings were built at Feering Halt, Brookland Siding, Inworth, Tiptree, Tudwich Road Siding, Tolleshunt Knights, Church Siding, Tolleshunt d'Arcy, Old Hall Siding, Tollesbury and Tollesbury Pier.

It was hoped at one time to establish a yachting station and continental port at Tollesbury. Hence the pier. The latter stood semi-derelict for many years. Part of it was blown up during the last war to prevent it being used by invaders. The final relics were swept away in the Great Tide of 1953. One has many memories of bitter nights and dawns, wildfowling on the freezing muds of the Blackwater or punt-gunning up Thurslet Creek or Mell Creek when the return to the tiny pier station meant that one could shelter from wind, sleet or snow for a few blessed minutes of comparative warmth.

The Crab and Winkle railway line was opened on October 1, 1904, when 120 people travelled to Tollesbury where they lunched at the King's Head. It died, deeply mourned, on Saturday, May 5, 1951. A funeral party of 450 mourners went from Kelvedon to Tollesbury on the last run. The engine and coaches were festooned with fluttering streamers and cheered on their way by blasts of fog-horns, football rattles and roars of applause.

A black coffin covered with wreaths lay on Tiptree station. On the engine's firebox was chalked "Born 1904 . . . Died 1951" and on the bunker was the solemn warning, "There be many a poor soul have to walk." So died a legend.

The River Blackwater at Kelvedon

Winged magic of the Essex shore

Birds that girdle the earth... magic of the Essex Oxbird... aerobatic wonders... the man who fought the pump... what goes into a 'sea pudden' ... curlew and other waders

Walk along the shore at Shoeburyness, Thorpe Bay, Southend, or better still, Leigh Marsh, Canvey Point, or that rich sanctuary of wildfowl the Tilbury shoreline, and you will see a cloud of smallbirds, no larger than sparrows but far more delicate in form. They have longer legs, longer beaks and a more stream-lined figure than the cocky little sparrow. These are the most remarkable small waders that fly. The reason is that they girdle the earth. Those tiny bodies powered by scimitar wings fly round the world. The birds you see skimming over the tide-edge from the end of Southend pier may well have been in Africa or India a week or so ago.

These little winged wonders are dunlin. Essex inshore fishermen and wildfowlers call them oxbirds. In Norfolk the coastal wildfowlers call them stints. Elsewhere they call them sealarks, or purres.

Now this engaging little bird is a form of sandpiper. The average length is seven-and-a-half inches, the wing length four-and-a-half inches, the general colouring dun—hence the name—black wing markings and white underside. The general effect, as you see them running along the shore like feathered mice, is of a little dusky coloured bird of infinite grace and activity.

Many of them nest in this country, but others in summer go to Northern Europe and Asia and down to the Mediterranean, India and Africa in winter.

The astonishing thing about dunlin is their amazing aerobatics. Almost the smallest bird, they not only fly the longest distance, but they are capable of the most amazing mass formation flying.

Watch them sweep up the coast, fling themselves suddenly skyward and then, as at a word of command, dive in ordered formation, down to the sea. They look like a shower of falling silver. Somewhere, among that twittering flight of small birds, is a Commander-in-Chief. Who else gives the order? By what means does he translate the message to those tiny brains when they turn like one? Their evolutions are among the most remarkable sights in the whole bird world. Unfortunately they are decreasing yearly. You may still see them in their thousands, but old Essex men lament the days when they were in their tens of thousands.

Years ago, a favourite dish among marshmen and gunners was "oxbird pudden". The cottage housewife patiently plucked two or three dozen of the tiny bodies precisely as she would patiently pluck two or three dozen sparrows for "sparrer pudden". I have eaten both and jolly good they are.

"Oxbird pudden" was made not only with the oxbirds themselves but with a lump or two of fat pork to give it flavour, the breasts of half-a-dozen moorhens — infinitely gamier than any pheasant — and any other oddment that fell to the gun, such as redshank - called tukies in Essex — sandpipers, grey plover or peewits. The result was delicious. "Oxbird pudden" as made by a village housewife, was a work of art of infinite flavour.

Almost as good was the "sea-pudden" made aboard some of the smacks in a bucket. Anything and everything went into that bucket, fish, fowl and eels. When that good Essex sportsman, the late Dr. Carl Gimson, used to go out fowling from Tollesbury at the end of the 1914-18 war, his skipper, crew and cook was a wonderful seaman whose name, alas, I forget. He could have sailed that big, beamy old smack from Essex to the Baltic and back again single-handed. But when it came to cooking a mixed pudden in a pail, he revealed a skill sublime. You will never get anything like it in the Savoy grill!

Another form of communal mass cooking in which oxbirds usually figured, were the gargantuan stews made by farm housewives on Foulness and in the Dengie Hundred before 1914 when the harvest labour was recruited from inland without much inquiring into the criminal, or other, records of the labourers. Many of them were Irish. On Saturday nights they would fight anything from the parish pump to the parish police. I remember one rustic tough who lurched out of the pub in the full moon, bumped into the parish pump, got a stunning blow from the spout in his solar plexus, and promptly drew off and then let fly with both flailing fists. He hammered the pump blow after blow until he had skinned his knuckles almost to the bone. Then he lurched off, bloody but unbowed, in search of a crowbar with which to fell his immovable enemy.

That was the type of man who, often on the run from the inland police, flocked in droves to the lonely marsh farms at harvest. They had to sleep in the barn or in the long dormitories which you find under the roof-trees of big old farmhouses round about Dengie and Tillingham. As someone wrote at the time: "They lived like hogs and fought like dogs".

Each man was supposed to bring his share of food to the farmer's wife. It could be anything from poached hare or a brace of rabbits to a bagful of waders, oxbirds included, which they had either shot on the tideline or taken in nets, set out across the mudflats just before the turn of the tide. Everything, hares, rabbits, dead piglets thrown on to the "muck dungle", fish, eels, birds, swedes and turnips, went into the gigantic stew which bubbled in a great iron pot over the open fire. Oxbirds were the ultimate delicacy.

Other waders which you will see along the Thamesmouth tideline include birds which are either too handsome to shoot or not worth shooting. The oyster-catcher, to beautiful to kill, too rank to eat - the "olive" of Essex, the St. Olaf's bird of the Norsemen; the turnstone, handsome in summer, confiding in winter; the "tangle-picker" of the Norfolk coast; the ring-dotterel or ring-plover and his first cousin, the Kentish plover, both tiny, waistcoated little people who will sometimes approach within arm's length, turning over seaweed and picking daintily at the sands as one waits motionless. I have seen many a ring-plover feed within a foot of my boot even when I have been walking on the sands.

But when we come to curlew, to golden, grey and green plover, to the dashing, piping redshank, to the whimbrel with his haunting whistle, the greenshank with his desolate cry, we come to the game birds of the shore - the birds who can well look after themselves, worthy fowl, worthy of one's wits and weapons.

Curlew are the wariest of all birds, wild geese excepted. They are large, handsome, good to eat, and carry away a lot of shot. Yet oddly enough the belief persists that a curlew, in spite of the ancient tag which "carries tenpence on her back", is almost unfit for food. This is quite wrong. A curlew fresh from the stubble fields in September, straight from the plough in October and November, is fit for any table. Properly cooked, it is an excellent bird.

The Count of the Essex shore

The French wildfowler who made salt water history . . . the last of the gentlemen gunners.

Essex has always either bred or attracted "characters". Standing in the corner of the gunroom is an Essex "sledge" gun which reminds me of such a man. It was used less than 100 years ago by an old Tollesbury fowler who mounted it on a mud-sledge which he pushed over the flats under the moon in order to shoot widgeon feeding along the tide-edge. The sledge was usually propelled by the fowler's feet, aided and guided by wooden hand-pads which he dug into the mud. The gun was given to me by the late Count de la Chapelle, a very dear friend and a great wildfowler and naturalist. There indeed was a "character".

Xavier Victor Alfred Octave de Morton, Count de la Chapelle, was a man from another age, a more coloured century. Born in 1863, the son of a Gascon aristocrat, who had been Court Chamberlain during the Third Empire, he was one of those rare men to whom life is a constant gallant adventure. He made friends for life when he made them at all. And his choice, usually, was for those who appealed to his own nature, a dashing Gascon temperament, that had no use for men who avoid risk, who have not lived dangerously.

For thirty-five years he lived a great deal at Tollesbury, where he owned and partly built a shooting-box known as Heron Lodge, surrounded by beautiful gardens. Here he kept his wonderful collections of weapons, armour, prehistoric and Napoleonic relics, and stuffed birds—all rare Essex specimens. Most of his ornithological collection is now preserved in my own small museum. Many of his weapons and flint implements are in Colchester Museum.

He was the head of an old French family who owned the Chateau de Montcuque in the country of Perigord, the country whence he inherited his appreciation of good wine and good cooking and the Chateau Giomer, a square and lonely house on the edge of the marshes of Saint-Valery-sur-Somme. There the late Count first learned the arts of wildfowling.

He began at the age of twelve with a pinfire twenty-bore gun, under the tutelage of an old fowler named Boyard, and a punt-gunner named Lamidel. Boyard taught him to shoot snipe on the fens of the Somme, to kill larks over a "twirler", to bring down hawks and owls to a Grand Duc Articule, to decoy duck and to shoot them on the "Huttier" system. From Lamidel he learned, amid the sandbanks and dangerous shallows of the Baie de la Somme, the management of small

The tall brick tower of St Andrew's Church Rochford, and the imposing higher stair turret

boats in short tides and choppy waters, the working of a punt gun, the art of digging in on the tide-line and shooting over decoys.

Then, when Napoleon II was banished from France, the Count's father preferred to follow his Emperor into exile rather than remain under a republic. The estates went, and with them went most of the land on which Paris Plage and Le Touquet are built. Then it was a sandy, pine-clad warren. Today it is worth a fortune.

He was descended on the female side from the Earls of Morton, one of whom was Regent of Scotland during the life of Mary Queen of Scots. Possibly from that far Scottish strain la Chapelle inherited that determination and forthrightness of character which led him to strike out for himself into the fields of international law, where he founded and became the head of a firm which handled many important cases and held many European secrets. He was legal counsellor to the Royal Rumanian Legation and once, I remember, stopped a duel which, had it ended fatally, might well have been the cause of another European war. He was sixty-four years of age but he stopped the duel by declaring, in a most un-lawyer-like manner, that if it was fought, he himself would challenge the victor.

As a swordsman he was brilliant in his younger days and one of the best pupils of Professor Magrini. But wildfowling and yachting were his principal sports. He was a founder and vice-president of the Wildfowlers' Association, owned a gunning-yacht for thirty-five years, and skippered her himself. He was no fair-weather yachtsman. His twenty-ton Scoter or the five-ton Teal were known all up the coast from Orford Ness to the Maplin Sands, and they were seen oftener at sea in winter than in summer.

I think, in his heart of hearts, he rather despised inland wildfowling. He was a true salt-water gunner of our real North Sea type, a sailor who loved a blow from the north-east.

From his early days of hunting for the pot among the Sioux Indians with their wild adventures or riding down the last of the bison, to the day of his death, his life was full of adventure.

Once during the 1914-18 war he was punting in the mists of a winter dawn on the Essex Blackwater. Suddenly out of the fog a destroyer swung into view, whistles sounded, orders were shouted, a gun was trained on them and a shell clanged home in the breech. He and his puntsman, Will Leavett, leapt to their feet and waved their arms. A second later and they would have been blown out of the water. The destroyer had

mistaken the long, low outline of the punt, with the two men sitting upright, the long gun in front of them, for the outline of a submarine, its gun the conning-tower.

Half an hour later, when he returned to the jetty at Tollesbury, he was arrested as a Geman spy! He was only released on the indignant expostulations of the local coastguard

The 'captains houses' facing the green at Harwich, an important port and link with the Continent

who identified him as "our very own Vice-Count". Inspite of this he insisted on returning to the estuary, where two hours later the punt narrowly escaped being blown out of the water by a depth charge.

One month later he brought about the arrest of an authentic spy, who was shot at the Tower.

He volunteered for active service as a Tommy at the age of fifty-one and was refused. It was just as well, for later he was largely responsible for bringing Rumania into the war on the side of the Allies.

A year or two previously when on a business visit to France he suddenly decided to revisit his native village of La Chapelle. He arrived late at night. Next morning he was wakened by the blowing of horns, the barking of dogs and the shouting of men. A boar hunt had been arranged in his honour. "But I have no clothes and no gun", he expostulated, pointing to his patent leather shoes and straw hat. The mayor soon remedied that. He clapped a fireman's helmet on the Count's head, thrust a rusty pinfire loaded with ball cartridge into his hand, and bade the "chasse" begin.

One of the guns was the village chemist, a large man in a Panama hat with a red silk cummerbund. Presently the boar was roused. A shot followed, then a scream. La Chapelle, in his fireman's helmet, gas-pipe in hand, advanced towards the screams. In a clearing he saw the chemist, hanging from a swaying sapling, his gun on the ground, his arms and legs wrapped about the tree. Every time the sapling swayed downward the chemist came within six feet of the ground, and each time the boar, a hoary, grey, red-eyed old tusker, charged. La Chapelle took aim, prayed that the gun might stand the charge, and fired, The right barrel mis-fired. The boar charged. The left barrel took him in the shoulder at fifteen feet, and he dropped dead. That was the end of the "chasse".

That night there was a banquet at the village inn. La Chapelle, still in his helmet, garlanded with roses, was crowned "Roi de La Chasse" and invited to kiss the head forester's pretty daughter.

I have a vivid recollection of him at the age of fifty-six hauling a burly taxi driver off his seat in the Cromwell Road and punching him on the nose because the man had used foul language in the presence of a lady.

But Octave was no swash-buckler. He merely had an eighteenth century mind. No man was a better host, a more appreciative guest, and a more ardent and tireless wildfowler. No day was too long, no weather too bitter, no discomfort

Old cottages and houses in Stebbing Green

The timbers in the Cressing Temple barns are said to date from the twelfth century. They were probably built by the Knights Templar but they were passed on to the Knights Hospitallers in the fourteenth century

This attractive grouping of houses has made Finchingfield one of the most photographed villages in Essex

Fishermen bringing in their boat at Clacton-on-Sea after a morning's outing

Attractive house and shop fronts in Great Dunmow High Street

The famous Paycocke's House in Coggeshall. Built by wool merchant Thomas Paycocke about 1500, the magnificently carved timbers, inside and out, make this one of the most attractive old houses in England

The tower keep at Castle Hedingham is one of the best preserved in England. It had been the seat of the Earls of Oxford, the de Vere family. The keep dominates the surrounding countryside, and can be seen from miles around

Delightful street scene at Newport, once an ancient, busy market town

too acute, when he was out in his little gunning yacht, the Teal, or in either of his two big punts, the Grebe and the Heron, which I took over when he gave up shooting.

His house, Heron Lodge, which stood above Woodrope Farm, overlooking the Blackwater, the Wick marshes and the wide saltings of Tollesbury Fleet, was a museum of weapons, trophies and the paraphernalia of the wildfowler. He had a wonderful collection of guns, ranging from a Holland and Holland breech-loading punt gun firing a pound of shot down through the whole gamut of four-bores, eight-bores, ten-bores, twelve-bores, and twenty-bores to a double four-ten.

The wildfowler who knows the Essex coast will be surprised that a man who owned all the accessories for punt-gunning and shore-shooting, who had time and money to spare, should have killed relatively few wild geese and duck. There are two reasons. The first was Octave was a romantic who scorned any form of wildfowling which was not, in his own phrase "salt-water gunning". He loved the perils and ardours of pursuing fowl in a punt or waiting for them, hour after hour in his favourite hide among the suaeda bushes on Shingle Head Point, or crouched in a freezing rill on the "Holes" as they call the Great and Little Cob Islands. During the many years when we knew each other I rented duck marshes, first-class and otherwise, at Langenhoe and Goldhanger, Mersea Island and Tollesbury. I grew tired of inviting him to shoot. It was useless.

"My dear boy, it is not salt-water gunning", with that quizzical smile, "it is too easy."

Only those who have walked ten to twenty miles in a day on an Essex marsh, jumped dykes, waded thigh-deep through stinking fleets, trodden Agag-like over quaking bogs and been out from the chill of dawn until the first wink of stars can realise how "easy" it is. But for Octave there was no real wildfowling once you were inside the sea wall.

The other reason why he shot relatively few geese and duck was that with his natural magnanimity of character he refused steadfastly to punt on any flats which he regarded as the natural shooting ground of the Maldon gunners and other local men who earned their living in winter with their punts and guns. It would have been easy for him to have sailed his yacht two or three miles from his headquarters towing his punt, to have anchored for the night and to have been in the middle of a vast gathering of brent and widgeon at the crack of dawn. He refused to do so.

"That ground belongs to the Pitts, or the Handleys, or the Claydons", he would say. "They have their living to earn.

Looking across the Blackwater from near Mill Point, Tollesbury

They have to row there. They only have muzzle-loaders to shoot with. Why should I steal a march on them?"

He received, in his last journey on earth, a spontaneous tribute from the fishermen and wildfowlers of that remote Essex coastal village which must, I think, have lightened his footsteps to the other Hunting Ground. Every house in the village had its blinds down, every shop was shuttered, no fishing smack set sail, as six sturdy sea captains and fishermen gunners, blue-jerseyed and thigh-booted, carried the coffin to a grave lined with sea lavender from the saltings he had loved.

And there, today, lies the last of the Gentlemen Gunners of the Blackwater Estuary, his feet to the North Sea, the salt wind blowing above him, the cry of the curlew and the white wings of gulls above him. In a grave, nearby, lies his old punter and life-long friend, Will Leavett, a man of like calibre. His ancestors came, I think, from Brittany, and were originally L'Evette. One night of sea fog and frost, the pair of them were out in the big punt Heron, off the mouth of Gunner's Creek on the Bradwell shore. It is just about the loneliest place on the East Coast, miles from anywhere and without any landmark to guide one home. The tide was coming in. The mist was rising. Suddenly out of the white mystery came a shuddering cry, "Oo! Oo! Oo! Save me, save me, O God, save me. Help! Help!" The ghostly cry echoed over the creeping tide. "Chippy" Leavett, whose other nickname was Too-Hoo, thought for an instant, as he told me afterwards, that the Devil had come to snatch him. Then he and Octave listened intently, heard the plop, plop of feet in the mud. The foosteps drew nearer. A figure loomed out of the mist. It was an old man, gun under arm, oil-skinned and thigh-booted, his face stricken with fear. They took him aboard the punt and rowed up the rill to an old barge permanently anchored in shallow water. There the old man lived alone with his dog. His name was D'Wit. One of a Mersea family of that name which still endure. They date from the days of the Dutch drainers. Becky D'Wit, who died in 1978, was one of the last breed. The old man with the gun was the hermit of the coast. He lived on the birds he shot and the fish he caught. That night Octave and Chippy saved the old man's life.

The Deer Parks of Essex

Some parks in the North-East of the county . . . Shirley's list . . . Whitaker's Survey in 1892 . . . Parks in 1594 . . . Hempstead, Henham, Maynards, Porters, Bradfield, Castle Hedingham, and Moynes . . . some mid-Essex parks . . . Thorndon, Weald, Belhus, Danbury and others . . . the strong stags of Thorndon and the black fallow deer of Wivenhoe.

A friend, a farmer's wife who lives within 100 yards of an Essex main road, regularly feeds two or three deer at her kitchen door. They come up to the house and look at her through the scullery window. Her father, who farms about 200 acres, reckons that he has some seventy-five to 200 or more wild fallow deer in his woods and fields. One day, not long ago, he and I counted seventy-five bucks, does and fawns lying in a hayfield not a quarter of a mile from the roar of London-bound traffic. We got within thirty yards of them in the Land Rover.

Later, when the the hay was cut, a tiny fawn, abandoned by its mother, was picked up and brought home. My daughter sat up in bed and cuddled it. A neighbouring farmer adopted it as a pet. It was suckled by a ewe in the barn and has grown up with the sheep.

Now this all pinpoints the fact that more deer are running wild in Essex today than at any time since the reign of Elizabeth I, when the Great Forest of Essex, which extended from London to Colchester, was alive with deer both red and fallow, wild boar, badgers and foxes.

Mention of the last two reminds me of the sad tale told me by an observant friend, the late Frank Harris of Poplars Farm, Brook Street, Brentwood. He counted no fewer than thirteen dead badgers and well over twenty foxes killed by motor cars on not more than a 200-yard stretch of the Brentwood bypass since it was opened a few years ago. Heaven knows how many others have been killed which escaped his notice. Deer also have been killed on the same stretch and again in Epping Forest and near Bishop's Stortford.

The truth is that up to the beginning of World War one Essex was studded with private deer parks.

(The late Evelyn Shirley of Ettington Park, near Stratford-on-Avon, a well-known antiquarian, wrote an erudite and very scarce book entitled *Some Accounts of English Deer Parks* about 100 years ago. I have a copy of it, and in it he says: "Several other parks are marked in Norden's survey of Essex, made in 1594. Hempstead, Horeham, Henham, Maynards, Porters, Bradfield, Bell House, Castle Hedingham and Moynes are in the north-western part of the county."

A restored weatherboarded watermill at Sible Hedingham

Horeham is mentioned by Leland in the following passage: "Old Cutte married the Daughter and Heyre of one Roodes. Old Cutte buildid Horeham-Haule, a very sumptuous house in Essex, by Thaxtede; and there is a goodly pond or lake by it and faire parkes there about." Bell House is said to have been enclosed by Sir Edward Bassett, knighted by James I. If so it must have been in the reign of Elizabeth I, as it is marked on both Norden's and Saxton's maps.

Castle Hedingham, "a very stately house, mounted on a hille, havinge three parkes" belonged to the Earls of Oxford, and in Elizabeth's time to Lord Burghley.

In the north-eastern parts of Essex other parks are given by Saxton. Four are marked in the neighbourhood of Colchester; at Wivenhoe, Elmstead, Grimsted and Mile End; that at Wivenhoe is an existing park of 150 acres of land, until recently, with a herd of 160 fallow deer. Four other parks appear in Saxton's survey; at Wickes or Wykes (Wix) or Park Hall, the ancient inheritance of the Bohuns in the parish of Bradfield; at Ockley Parve; and two at "Clackton".

In the south-eastern division of Essex, besides the parks at Rochford and Rayleigh there was one belonging to the castle of Hadleigh or Hadley, where Christopher Barton and John Trevelyan were appointed keepers in 1446, and there were others at Beches and at Danbury, once the ancient seats of the Mildmay family.

Shirley was wrong when he put Bell House and Bradfield "in the north-western part of the county." Bell House was clearly Belhus, for generations the seat of the Barrett-Lennard family near Aveley on the Thames estuary, while Bradfield is near Manningtree overlooking the Stour estuary.

As a child I had lively hero-worship for the late Sir Thomas Barrett-Lennard of Belhus, since to my young eyes he was the epitome of manly vigour. He would drive out from the Hall in the morning in a pair-horse carriage with a coachman, go round the estate of 3691 acres calling on farmers and cottagers, who all adored him, and then, when four or five miles from home, chuck his coat into the carriage and run home behind it all the way. Thus he kept fit. Can you see any of our modern take-over tycoons curing their swag bellies by trotting home behind the expense-account Rolls?

Shirley listed the following Essex deer parks as those containing deer in 1867: Audley End, Lord Braybrooke; Thorndon, Lord Petre; Wivenhoe, Mr. Gurdon-Rebow; Weald Hall, Mr. Tower; Bell House, Sir Thomas Barrett-Lennard, Bart.; Easton, the Hon. Miss Maynard; Hallingbury, Mr. Archer Houblon; Braxted, Mr. Ducane; Langleys, Mr. Tufnell; Bore-

ham, Sir John Tyrell, Bart.; Shortgrove, Mr. Smith.

Evelyn Shirley, who owned 26,386 acres in Co. Monaghan in Northern Ireland and 2404 acres at Ettington in Warwickshire, of a gross annual value of £23,744, was that now rare bird the country gentleman who is not only a practical man of the land but also a classical scholar, a genealogist, an historian, something of an artist and a Member of Parliament. He did everything well and gracefully.

The spectacular parapet at the church at Earls Colne is studded with the badge of the de Vere family, Earls of Oxford, many of whose members were buried here. Above the parapet is a gilt ironwork crown for a weathervane

A man of much of the same calibre was the late John Whitaker, of Rainworth Park, Nottinghamshire. Both he and Shirley published books on deer parks and travelled hundreds of miles to visit various parks. Shirley made another little niche in history for himself by compiling that scarce and frequently illuminating volume *The Noble and Gentle Men of England*. In it he pins down firmly the pedigrees of "the families now existing (i.e. in 1860) and regularly established either as knightly or gentle houses before the commencement of the sixteenth century." It was a book that caused a lot of heart-burning then and still serves to puncture a few puffed-up people who imagine that the length of their purses offsets the shortness of their pedigrees—not, one imagines, a bedside book of the "half county" types.

Whitaker did not bother himself with debunking human pretensions. He was a naturalist first and foremost, an historian of ancient parks and duck decoys. This caused him to pay many visits to Essex. In the latter years of his life I was able to help him with details of certain now-vanished Essex decoys. In turn he gave me a great deal of information on Essex deer parks as he knew them in the 1800s. The following was his concise, descriptive summary of Essex deer parks in 1892.

Easton Park. Owner, Lady Brooke (later Countess of Warwick). Acreage 700. Fence, part wire, part close-paled. Water supply, natural. Number of fallow deer, 450. Average weight of bucks, 18 stone of 8 lb. Average weight of does, 10 stone. Number of red deer, 120. Average weight of stags, 25 stone. Average weight of hinds, 14 stone. Other animals, a herd of fifty goats. Well timbered and watered; holds many fine oaks. Rather flat.

Hatfield Forest Park. Owner, G.B. Archer Houblon, Esquire. Acreage 500. Fence, wire. Water supply, natural. Number of fallow deer, 300. Average weight of does 60 lb. Average weight of bucks, 104 lb. Number of red deer, ten. Average weight of stags, one 20 stone; none killed. Heavy land, clay. Trees, oak, ash, etc. oak very fine. Flat, well timbered; some enclosed game coverts in the park; ponds, rather wild. It was till recent times a forest. (It is now open to the public.)

Thorndon Hall. Owner, Lord Petre. Acreage, north park about 341, south park about 373. Fence, oak park fencing. Water supply, natural and plentiful. Number of fallow deer, about fifty. Number of red deer, about forty. Pheasants and other game. Timber very fine, park undulating and scenery varied and picturesque. Fine views are obtained from the house over the Thames, the Kent hills, etc. A large herd of deer about 1,200 strong was killed down some few years ago after the destruction by fire of the mansion. A new herd of each kind is now being raised, and is at present confined to the north park. The red deer have always been fine animals, and masters of hounds who had them for hunting purposes used to say that the Thorndon deer as a rule ran better before hounds than any others.

Weald Park. Owner, Christopher J.H. Tower, Esquire. Acreage 300. Fence, close pale and strained wire fencing. Water supply, two lakes and a small stream. Number of fallow deer, eighty. Average weight of bucks, 14 stone of 8 lb. Number of red deer, seventy. Average weight of stags, 20 stone of 14 lb. clean cut with head and skin as in Scotland. Nine Japanese deer (Cevus sika) and two roe. Very fine old oak and hornbeam timber; large amount of fern, five to six feet high in places. (Weald Hall is now pulled down, the estate broken up and the Towers, the best type of squire, have gone. Fortunately the park is owned by the County Council, open to the public, and still carries a fair herd of deer.)

Belhus Park. Owner, Sir Thomas Barrett-Lennard, Bart. Acreage, about 300. Fence, wooden park palings. Water supply, natural. Number of fallow deer about 100 now, formerly 300. Average weight of bucks, 14 stone of 8 lb. Average weight of does, 9 stone. Other animals, horses, cattle and sheep. About seven acres of water and several small ponds; a great many trees, oak, elm, lime, beech, etc. This park has the ancient and now uncommon right of free warren.

Mark Hall Park (near Coggeshall). Owner, Mrs. Honywood. Acreage 200. Fence, close-paled. Water supply, natural. Number of fallow deer, 200. There are fine oaks, thorns, limes etc.

Wivenhoe Park. Owner, H.J. Gurdon-Rebow, Esquire. Acreage 180. Fence pale fence, three miles outside, iron fencing inside. Water supply, natural and artificial. Number of fallow deer, about 100, all black. Average weight of bucks, 96 lb. dead weight. Average weight of does, 60 lb. dead weight. Fine old oaks between 400 and 500 years old, limes, elms and beeches. Eighty acres of ferns, four acres of ornamental water and a brook intersect the park, forming the boundary between Greenstead and Wivenhoe parishes. (Wivenhoe is now the site of the unlovely Essex University. The black deer have gone with the wind.)

Langleys Park. Owner, J.J. Tufnell, Esquire. Acreage 100. Fence, partly oak and partly iron. Water supply, natural, the River Chelmer and brook running into the river. Number of fallow deer, eighty-eight. Average weight of bucks, 13 stone. Average weight of does, 8 stone. Good timber, both in the park and in the park-like lands adjoining.

Quendon Park. Owner, Lieutenant Colonel A.M. Cranmer-Byng; Acreage about eighty or ninety. Fence, old-style wood and part wire. Water supply, two ponds. Number of fallow deer, about 100. Some very fine oaks. Has been a deer park for about 200 years.

The number of deer which have escaped from many parks that have been dis-parked, is difficult to compute. It is enough to say that Essex today has more deer running wild than it has had for some hundreds of years past. Deer turn up on many farms and in gardens when they are least expected. They add beauty to the County and do very little damage to farm crops. As the late Frank Harris remarked: "I like to see them about and I would never grudge them a dinner. They are part of old Essex."

Lord Petre's Hounds

The story of an historic pack . . . the peer who hunted like a prince . . . some old Essex hunting families

The house stands warmly red in the sun, old and demure, on the left of the road from Brentwood to Herongate. Just this side of the Dairy Farm, which as you know, is opposite the Priests' House, hidden in its shrubberies on the edge of Thorndon Park.

The tall chimneys and gaunt facade of that Palladian Pentonville, one of the unlovelier works of Paine, gazes across the park to the little red house by the roadside standing back in its garden in the bright fields. They call it the Huntsman's House. And as such I knew it first in 1914 when the park beyond the high brick wall and the deep ha-ha, was then full of the tall deer, dappled in the bracken.

Today, Thorndon Park, like many another great estate, has been broken up, the sense of continuity gone, the sluttish fingers of the bungalow developer clawing at its tattered skirts. That is the price we pay for death duties, the most immoral tax ever devised by man, since it puts a premium on the inevitability of death, and destroys the toil, thought and care of centuries of good ownership. Luckily the great house itself has been turned into flats of stately grace which revive the old grandeur.

That little red house by the road is a monument of past glories. For there, from 1822 to 1832, if indeed not earlier, the Lord Petre of the day housed his huntsman and kennelled his hounds. His father before him kept hounds at Thorndon Hall before 1822, but I cannot discover the date when the pack was first got together. The interesting point is that it was the forerunner of the present Essex Union. Lord Petre had a second period of mastership from 1836 to 1839.

Bailey's Hunting Directory, that crimson bible of the foxhunter, tells us no more than a few lines about Lord Petre's hounds, but lately, looking through a run of that defunct sporting magazine, *Bailey's* which I had from the library at Noblethorpe Hall near Wentworth Woodhouse in Yorkshire, I came across a very full account by an anonymous writer, printed in December 1874, over a hundred years ago.

It is worth giving in full since it is part of Essex history and will, I think, awaken many memories, not only among old sportsmen but in the minds of many young men and women of today whose fathers and grandfathers rammed down their hats and hardened their hearts when Lord Petre's hounds went away on a breast-high scent.

Our unknown author says:

These hounds hunted the country up to Southend, Mal-

Fishing for the family — in a sylvan setting in Thorndon Park

The sun blazes down and lights up part of Thorndon Park

don and Chelmsford, a very rough one and I may say, nearly or quite, all plough. The fences are large, being generally a high bank with a stiff hedge or a big ditch on one side or the other and occasionally on both; consequently it is a strong country to ride over and very deep, but few ploughs when the land gets settled, carry a better scent than those of the Essex Union.

The history of this country and that of the South Essex are so bound together that it is not easy to make out their modern history separately.

The first Master was Mr. Jesse Russell of Stubbers, near South Ockenden, and his Huntsman was John Stevens who afterwards lived at Hornchurch and dealt a little in horses. He died at the great age of ninety-three. His son, the celebrated Jack Stevens, whipped-in to him before he went to Lord Middleton in Warwickshire and became so well known with Mr. Osbaldeston in the Quorn country.

Mr. North Surridge of Rainham, a gentleman farmer and banker at Romford, hunted that portion of the country afterwards called the South Essex for some time, several years before Lord Petre kept foxhounds. He managed the hounds three or four seasons with a subscription, and earned the gratitude of the country being hunted at all after the retirement of the predecessor, Mr. Harding Newman, or as he was generally called, Newman. Newman, it is said, hunted the Romford, Stifford and Laindon Hill country and on to Billericay and Norsey Wood, between Mr. Russell's and Mr. North Surridge's time.

About 1821 or 1822, the late Lord Petre took the South Essex country, having his kennels at Thorndon Hall near Brentwood, and he hunted it regularly up to 1831. The country during that time was bounded on the south and east side by the Thames from Dagenham to the port of Maldon. The mail-coach road from London to Colchester was the northern boundary as far as Chelmsford and from thence to Maldon a small river defined its limits. There was, however, one exception: near Ingatestone and on the north side of the before-mentioned road the Blackmore Highwoods, Edney Wood and Writtle Park, a large portion of which woodlands belonged to Lord Petre, were hunted by him, neutrally, with Mr. Conyers.

The Blackmore Highwoods I believe then consisted of 1,300 acres, 900 of which belonged to Lord Petre. There were rare useful woodlands, generally holding a good scent and but few hares and always producing a fox when called on. To these coverts Lord Petre would take the whole of his young hounds at once in September, for they could do no harm there; and they frequently ran for hours from fox to fox, sometimes getting blood, sometimes missing it, but invariably getting work enough with their legitimate game to do them much good.

Lord Petre hunted the country in princely style, was a good judge of both horse and hound, and devotedly fond of both. In the early part of his career, there was a great variety of blood in the Thorndon Kennel, but for the last five or six years an annual draft of young hounds from Badminton was added to the selected home bred ones, so that long before his Lordship retired, the Beaufort blood largely predominated.

Master and men were always well mounted, the horses coming from Mr. Anderson of Piccadilly, who considered his Lordship quite his best customer. Lord Petre was a galloper, but rather a shy fencer. His groom, in scarlet, always rode with him, and his horses were made very handy to turn over the big banks and yawning ditches with which this country is intersected; so that if he did not ride close to hounds, he generally contrived to be near enough to see what was going on.

No man could enjoy a good run with a kill more than he did; and after a good ride, he would invariably ride home with the hounds, never omitting to give the men some bread and cheese on the way, and if on his favourite Dandy, would indulge him with a quart of ale which he drank out of a bowl. He was particularly cheery, jocular, affable and kind, seldom speaking harshly to anyone though he could "come out" on occasions. This and his generosity, which was conspicuous, and hunting the country entirely at his own expense, made him very popular; moreover he was the best and kindest of masters.

The following letter, written to a second whip, announcing his intention of giving up the hounds, shows the kind feeling which existed between him and his servants:

'Bill—I am grieved at being obliged to tell you that the largeness of my family obliges me to give up the hounds. I am obliged to write this, for I cannot speak it, as it cuts me deep. I shall be happy to assist you in getting another place.'

The above was addressed to Mr. William Stansby, afterwards so many years at Badminton, who has carefully preserved this letter. His deputy steward or bailiff paid the servants' board wages monthly, and at the end of the season, he paid them their yearly salary himself, sending for them one by one, and never omitting to add an extra five-pound note.

The following story thoroughly shows his Lordship's goodness of heart: A farmer whose generosity was far in excess of his annual income, got into difficulties and amongst the necessary curtailments, the hunter had to be sold and considerable reductions made. Matters were arranged for his keeping on the farm—which I think had once been his own—but having now no horse to ride, he was miserable. Lord Petre sent for him, gave him a good horse, and told him to send for a quarter or two of good oats to finish the season. His eldest son was soon after in the 2nd Life Guards, and was for some time a rough-rider.

Apart from its connections with the aristocracy, Thorndon Park has also known and housed some unusual characters.

There was the remarkable story of the itinerant knife-grinder and his wife who lived for years in a tiny hut, built of corrugated iron, hidden in a wooded dell in the Park. For years, although visitors roamed the park, golfers stalked over the golf course, picnickers unpacked their baskets by the roadside and small boys swarmed like rabbits from the ever-growing nearby housing development, no-one, apparently, saw or suspected the humble, home-made ramshackle dwelling of the gypsy-like couple who lived their quiet, secret lives without gas, without piped water, without electric light, without a kitchen cooker—in fact without any of the comforts and gadgets which make the modern home.

Their ceiling was the stars by night, the sun or rain clouds by day. The owl and the nightingale were their pop-singers and the thrush and cuckoo their alarm calls in the dawn. The sly and stealthy fox and the old grey badger grunting on his nightly rounds or screaming like a murdered child, were their familiars. And, no doubt, rabbits and pheasants, mushrooms and blackberries, the nut plantation and the goat-eyed hare paid their toll to the pot which simmered on a fire of brushwood and cones.

The remarkable thing is that here we had, within a rifle shot of the Ford Motor Company's giant headquarters, within sound of the commuters' trains and the roar of main road traffic, a couple living lives almost as primitive as the Saxon foresters lived when Hereward the Wake defied William the Conqueror—and defeated him more than once—in 1066.

I knew another man of simple ways and ancient skills who lived near the earth and the trees and thereby possessed some strange, inborn, sixth sense of a sort denied to those who walked the pavements of the town. He was a hurdle-maker. He lived in a roadside cottage up Hanging Hill Lane not far from the twin villages of Herongate and Ingrave which cluster under the park belt of Thorndon.

When Thorndon was the heart of the great 19,100 acre estates of Lord Petre, there was plenty of work for the hurdle-maker. The Home Farm and the tenants' farms all ran sheep. Hurdles were an everyday necessity. Today the art of the hurdle-maker turns more and more to the making of wattle fencing.

Day by day the old man turned out a regular number of hand-made hurdles. The quantity seldom varied.

Then one day, without saying a word to his family, he doubled the output. He worked longer hours, often by lantern-light. The woodyard was stacked with rows of hurdles. They grew to an enormous stock-pile.

Finally his son, who told me the story, said, "Dad, why are you workin' so hard?".

"I'm going to be laid up, boy," said the old man, "For two months, maybe three. I feel it a'comin'. When I'm laid by you can sell them hurdles reglar every week. That'll keep the family afloat."

A month later the prophecy came true. The old man was desperately ill for weeks. Each week a regular quantity of hurdles went out and the money came in. Then the old hurdle-maker recovered—precisely to the day when the last batch of hurdles had been sold. His work went on.

Thorndon Hall during conversion into luxury flats.

Audley End ~ the jewel of Essex

Great sweep of unspoiled country . . . the Webster 'Home Pub' . . . perfect symmetry of a unique house . . . a great mansion.

North West Essex is a noble, unknown land. Noble because it is down-land country where the soft well of uplands meets the sky and the landscape glows with wheat and barley and is dappled by sheep and cattle. It has an air of space. Time stands still. History watches one. That which was yesterday lives on today. One feels that pre-history and early history, medievalism and the quiet splendours of Tudor and Georgian England merge naturally into each other.

A countryside of great estates, of yeomen farmers, whose ancestries often enough far outlast the family trees of some of the opulent city gents who in the last hundred years or less have bought old lands and old houses, and set themselves up as country gentlemen. Gradually the land absorbs them. The villages which for centuries have known the older gentry with their rooted values and quiet courtesy gradually tame the loud-voiced assertiveness of those who think that money buys everything and that if you hunt on Saturdays you are automatically a country gentleman. England has digested and absorbed their like in successive waves over the centuries. Earlier merchants, whether of stocks and shares, wool or wine, coal or beer, escaped from London to the sane peace of such quiet villages, old farms and manor houses of grace, and in them reared families who thereby gained new values of old worth and quiet sanity.

I forget who it was that said that with few exceptions, no great merchant families of the City of London had ever flourished for more than three generations without decline and decay. Hence, no doubt, the instinctive urge to leave the pavement for the ploughed field.

This great sweep of unspoiled country whose centre is, shall we say, Saffron Walden, has, with the adjoining Roothings, attracted many such newcomers and, in course of time, has absorbed them into its own quiet ways. Many an old cottage whose roof timbers were open to rain and wind, many an old farmhouse, moated, forlorn and alone, and more than one noble country house has been saved by Londoners with an eye for beauty and an inherited urge to live and sleep in rural peace.

One result today is that in many villages, especially in the Roothings, and this Essex Down country, the villages which one remembers fifty years ago as run down or half empty are today bright with old cottages and larger houses, once forlorn and now restored and reborn.

A splendid, ancient timbered cottage at Great Chesterford

I think with particular affection of an old moated manor house of red brick and timber called Colville Hall which sits demurely at the end of a farm lane. Pevsner describes it perfectly as "an exquisite piece of its type". And so it is. I remember it many years ago when it was rather run down and wished to be left alone. It was, however, never a ruin and never lost its feet off the land. Today the owners, Captain

Charles Webster, one time Dragoon Guards, and his wife, a portrait artist of quiet distinction, farm 120 acres including thirteen acres of woodland, and breed Jacob sheep, the oldest breed of sheep in the world, as well as horses and as many poultry, ducks and guinea fowl as the foxes will allow. They do it all with the help of one farm hand and one girl groom who looks after the Hunters which graze benignly in the green fields with the Tudor brick arched gateway. Charles Webster, in addition, conducts the family wine business with half a dozen or so solid looking family pubs on the Eastern fringes of London and that superb Tudor gem The Old Dr. Butler's Head, up a narrow street behind the Mansion House. There you can get the true old English cooking which our grandsires knew.

Leave London for Harlow which straddles the boundary between Essex and Hertfordshire and you come to the old Harlowbury Manor House which gazes with dignity over a village green. That is the Webster Head Office. The antithesis of the modern brash commercial office prison of concrete, formica and plate glass.

Round the corner, sitting astride a trout stream, Old Harlow Mill, the Webster 'Home Pub' should have been painted by Constable, and in age and good cooking matches the Old Dr. Butler's Head. There is an old room at the back of the mill behind the front parlour which has a warm human personality. It has the sense of being used and loved by many generations of people. A room of character. From the oak beams with their iron hooks they hung their hams and the Miller his double barrelled shot-gun. Step out through this room on to a balcony and you see the mill tail, with trees and meadows that have changed very little over the centuries. A little bit of Saxon England. Men stood here 1,000 years ago and drank their ale to the quack of ducks and the gurgle of the water in the dusk. An unchanging view, an avenue of water with trees on either side and always the whistle and gurgle of the mill race, white flecked, racing down to Bow and the Thames on its journey to the sea. This is a snug little corner of its own where one can sit and drink port and philosophise.

Looking north to Cambridgeshire, you can see a small fleet of punts and rowing boats for those wishing to escape the fettle snares of life and feed clamorous ducks of various breeds. On the other side of the mill pool there stands a group of poplars. This backwater has much of the warmth of the River Cam at Cambridge but far more variety.

The mill is a mixture of Georgian, Tudor and eighteenth century architecture and looks much the same as it did in

1861 even though it has changed owners four times. The first owners were the monks of Harlowbury. There is a haunted room in the attic. Roman relics were found nearby. These are now in Harlow Museum. The River Stort joins up with the mill stream down the avenue of water, canopied with leafy branches. An idyllic setting.

Let us strike north from this comely house of good food and wine to the grandest stately home of them all — Audley End. It is the stateliest house of its type in all England. It has none of the monotonous grandeur of Wentworth Woodhouse, the largest private house in England, or of Wentworth Castle, its neighbour, built to rival it. It does not seek to ape the cold palace style of Blenheim or the heavy majesty of Holkham, which like many great houses, do not fit into the English countryside, but tower above it.

Audley End is an almost unique blend of the warmer types of architecture which have left their lasting imprint on the English scene. It sits in a stately park above a confiding little stream. It has an air of perfect symmetry. You feel that

A famous group of old houses in Saffron Walden dating from the fourteenth and fifteenth century

92

it has seen the centuries pass and drawn lasting loveliness from them all. It has belonged to a King, Charles II, who never quite finished paying for it, to a Lord Treasurer who spent a vast fortune on it, to the Earls of Suffolk and to the Lords Braybrooke, all of whom, except Charles, were connected by blood. The original building was on the site of the old Abbey of Walden. The house was started by the First Earl of Suffolk, Lord Treasurer, head of the Howard family. He began building in 1603 and went on until 1616. He told King James it cost £200,000 - an immense sum in those days. The King dryly remarked that "it is too large for a King, but might do for a Lord Treasurer." Suffolk named the house after his maternal grandfather Thomas Audley, Speaker of the Reformation Parliament, who was given the Abbey of Walden in 1538 on the dissolution of the monastries. He lived for a time at Walden Abbey. On his widow's death, the property passed to Margaret, their younger daughter. She died in 1563 and the old house passed to her second husband Thomas Howard, fourth Duke of Norfolk, who was beheaded on Tower Hill in 1572 for his part in the Ridolfi Plot. His eldest son, Thomas Howard, succeeded to the Walden estate. He was a good soldier and was called to Parliament as Baron Howard de Walden in 1597, a title which still exists. Later he became Earl of Suffolk in 1603. In 1614 he was made Lord High Treasurer of England which provoked King James' remark about him being able to afford to build the forerunner of the present house. He determined to build a house which in size and grandeur would surpass any other private house in the Kingdom. He ordered a model house embodying his plan to be made of wood in Italy at a cost of £500. The plans went ahead on a grandiloquent scale. It nearly broke the Suffolk finances. The first, second and third Earls found that the upkeep of the enormous mansion drained their resources to the bone. It was a white elephant. Charles II at one time took a fancy to the house and offered to buy it for £50,000. He had not fully paid the money when the house was sold back to the fifth Earl in 1701.

Today the house looks like a palatial Jacobean palace. It is, in fact, a little more than 200 years old anywhere, and much smaller than the original. The actual creator of the house as we know it was Field Marshal Sir John Griffin Griffin. He was the nephew of Lady Portsmouth, one of the Howard family, who bought the house (partly a ruin), from the Earl of Effingham, also a Howard, for the ridiculous sum of £3,000 in 1751. She thought of turning the decayed house into a silk factory.

An M.P. in six Parliaments, Griffin Griffin became the

fourth Lord Howard de Walden in 1784, and later Baron Braybrooke of Braybrooke. He was Lord Lieutenant of Essex in the same year and Vice-Admiral of Essex in 1795. He was clearly a man of enormous energy, determination and vision. Today's mansion is his splendid monument. He restored the best of its classic architecture without destroying the warmth and dignity of the living quarters. The house had been reduced in size but what remains is still a great mansion. It is the architectural jewel of Essex.

Today Audley End is in the custody of the Ministry of Public Building and Works who treat it as a national treasure. And so it is. The pictures, furniture and other contents belong to Lord Braybrooke's son, the Hon. Robin Neville, by whose permission they are on view. Thus the reborn old house still retains the air of being lived in. One of the star exhibits of the place which draws field sportsmen and naturalists is the superb collection of stuffed birds and animals, British and foreign.

The original landed estate still surrounds the house and is one of the best shoots in England. Nearby villages have kept their looks and their souls. There is an indefinable aura of the older England. I had a taste of this when I went to shoot at Heydon, not far off. Sometimes one feels on entering a strange house or a hitherto unknown village that one has been there before. That day the sense of having seen it all before was overpowering. I said so to my host, a local yeoman farmer. "You should know it," he said with a smile. "Your mother's family the Asplands, were Lords of the Manor here between three and four hundred years ago. They held the Manor by the serjeantry of holding at the Coronation a silver basin of water in which the Monarch could wash his hands after the ceremony."

That is true but no one knows what those early ancestors did with the basin. Incidentally, the downland slope on which we stood that day was dug out in broad terraces on the lynchet system by pre-historic men who farmed it with more wisdom than we give them credit for. A Georgian sale catalogue described that particular parish as being famous for its flocks of Great Bustards. This, the largest of the British game birds, was as big as a turkey, long legged with broad barred fantail, long whiskers on either side of its face. It was coursed with hounds by men who rode as though foxhunting and was extremely good to eat. They became extinct less than a hundred years ago. Audley End knew them as a noble survival. That is true also of the house itself.

Saffron Walden has one of the largest parish churches in Essex. Lying in a commanding position, it is a most impressive church by all standards

Mersea

The Roman Isle where the Danes set up a pocket kingdom . . . the best oysters in the world . . . the coastline of ghosts . . . the island Queen of yesterday . . . a temple of Lucullus.

When Edwardian yachtsmen sailed the luminous Essex seas in gaff-rigged cutters, the Social and Sailing Club on Mersea Island was a humble boatshed with its feet in the tide. It stood on the foreshore, smelling of tar and shavings, its black timbers bleached by salty winds. Its face looks south over shining creeks and marshes. And beyond, the river of the Dane, three miles wide, a great seaway.

Hastings, the Dane, laid up his longships in the broad creek which ebbs and flows, musical with curlew, in front of the old boatshed. There the Viking fleet, with shield-hung sides, dipped and rose on the tides, all through those long years from 893 until Alfred the Great drove them out. The Romans called this island Meresaia, "The Isle of the Sea". It was a petty principality of the sea reivers, a place cut off from England. It is still cut off. England crouches half a mile away, behind the hairy sea-walls of endless cattle marshes.

Another island, a whaleback of bleached grasses and wind-twisted thorn trees, rises out of the mud and the chuckling tides, the isle they call the Ray, where no man lives because, they say, the ghost of a Roman centurion walks at night with clanging footsteps.

The Romans had a camp on Mersea, a tall watch tower and a signal station to tell the garrison of Othona at Bradwell when a Viking warship came on the skyline. They built a causeway which we call the Strood from England to Mersea so that the garrison was mobile. It made Mersea a sea fortress for Romans and Danes alike.

It is an island of ghosts. Two warriors said to be Romans, fought to the death on Barrow Hill, now a farm hen run on the left side of the road to East Mersea. The clang of their swords cuts the silence of nights of moon. A few years ago archaeologists burrowed into this great mound which is 110 feet wide and 20 feet high. They found a small chamber 18 inches square and 21 inches high built of Roman bricks. In it was a small square lead casket. It contained a glass bowl just under a foot high. In it were the cremated remains of a grown-up person. It is now in Colchester Museum. They may be the remains of Hastings the Dane, who I believe lived in a Roman villa where West Mersea Church now stands. That church is largely built of Roman tiles. It was originally the Roman temple of Vesta.

It was at East Mersea Point that the Royalist guns were

97

Smugglers Way is the name of this cottage at West Mersea

Previous page: Sailing off the Essex coast near Mersea Island

the outer sea defences of Colchester in the Civil War. It was here in Victorian days that the parson, the Rev. Sabine Baring-Gould wrote that best selling melodrama *Mehalah*. Mehalah lived on Ray Island and was courted by a local ruffian who dwelt on Old Hall Marshes. Their blood-chilling courtship ended in a suicide pact at sea off East Mersea. It is still a book worth reading.

So do you wonder that this isle of Mersea, which is five miles long, a mile wide and contains five thousand acres, is a mighty independent sort of a place. Mersea men take no truck from anyone. Their forbears were smugglers and privateersmen. They manned the guns at Aboukir and were in that great fight with the Dutch when the Suffolk cornfields thudded all day to the thunder of the guns off Sole Bay.

They grow the best oysters in the world. They breed some of the finest skippers.

Mersea men live by the sea and the land, by the plough and the net, the gun and the tiller.

Now this island, as you might guess, had a Queen—a Queen of the cooking-pot, an insular Mrs. Beeton, a high priestess of the palate. She was more. She was a woman of quick wit, of Elizabethan tongue, of robust repartee, of great character in an island of character.

Generals paid court to her. Admirals came ashore to get a good meal. Writers and artists, particularly artists, for this is a land-and-sea place of bright and changing colours, were among her first lieges. And, on dark nights, silent, jerseyed men in seaboots, their faces graven with the watermarks of wind and salt spray, stalked quietly to her back door, long guns under their arms, slinking dogs at their heels and heavy gamebags on their shoulders. They dumped them on the kitchen floor for the queen to take toll in kind of fish and flesh and fowl. The pot was always on the boil.

She dwelt, as you might guess, in that old boatshed. A flagstaff at her front door. A look-out balcony to tell if the smugglers had come alive again. Within, the tar and shavings have gone. The black ship's beams, the high-pitched roof, the wide fireplaces remain. Ships's riding lights glowed green and red to port and starboard. The whips and cart harness, the bridles and horse brasses of the old hooded carriers' carts, which once lurched across the seaweed-green stones of the Strood, bringing rum and the week's letters out of England, hung on the wall.

And there was much else—all the pretty, sentimental junk from oyster smacks and deep-sea yachts, from merchant ships and fowlers' guns, with seascapes and cartoons by men whose brushes and pencils are famous.

For it was a club. A very English sort of club. You might have met Lord Goddard, who loved the place, or a peerless artist of the sea such as Syd Harnack who still lives nearby, a novelist such as Victor Bridges or Mr. Bert Thomas, whose cartooning fun is as English as the climate can make it. Or a deep-sea skipper, who has sailed the Seven Seas from the red rocks of Teneriffe to Amboina, the scented isle, or Guam, lonely on the Pacific horizon. The sort of rough and polished Englishman in whom old John Evelyn would have delighted when he was writing his scholarly Carolean Diary. You would find them telling the same sort of tale, quipping the same sort of quips that Nathaniel Hone would have put into his *Everyday Book* or his *Dictionary of Quotations*. That was just as it should have been. For this island queen, the late Mrs. Winifred Mary Hone, was a direct descendant of old Evelyn and, by marriage, of Nathaniel Hone.

The Hone family silver decorated her dining-room where you could have sat down on a winter's eve to a meal which Professor Saintsbury might bless, on which the shade of the vanished Boulestin might have gazed benignly, to which Brillat-Savarin might have given a culinary accolade.

A meal of hare soup and creamed oysters, of roast wild goose, lordly among its garnishings of grilled tomatoes, crisp fried potatoes, boiled samphire and giblet gravy. Or you could eat, as I have eaten, roast swan or a dish of golden plover, roasted on a spit, or widgeon, fresh shot from the tide; woodcock or curlew; or, if your mind turned to fish, eels of all sorts; soles, fresh from the estuary; or a mighty lobster, such as that leviathan, weighing fourteen pounds, which I helped to demolish. All that came to the pot went in it, and emerged, blessed.

During the war, seagulls went into a pudding, and men ate them, full of praise. There were rooks in the casserole; sparrows in a brisk brown pie; and, once, a heron, which a man shot and ate, fishily.

Eat a wild goose, flown straight from the oven, a greylag, a pinkfoot, a brent or a Canada goose, served with sauce made of cranberries, apples, oranges or gooseberries—once she concocted a sauce from the young shoots of broom—and you dined in style beneath the boathouse timbers.

Do you wonder that when Sir Winston Churchill came down to those parts to inspect troops, when the island's night skies were patterned with the fantastic geometry of searchlights, when bombs thudded down and the old boathouse timbers bent inwards beneath the blast like the sides of a drum, that the General Commanding sent his A.D.C. to the island Mrs. Beeton to beg that she would choose and cook the dinner for the greatest Englishman of our age?

It is all of a piece that the Commodore of this unique club should have been the late "Admiral" Bill Wyatt, boat-builder and descendant of Elizabethan shipwrights, winner for half a century of the annual smack race and a mighty man with a duck gun. He would tell you he had drunk eighteen thousand gallons of beer in his lifetime—"enought to float a tidy-sized smack"—and he once lassoed from his duck punt a ten-foot porpoise which towed him out to sea and back again before he beached it and found that it weighed a ton.

The "Admiral's" A.D.C., Bob South, is son of Old Bob who crossed the Atlantic seventeen times in racing yachts, whilst young Bob himself slew no less than nine wild geese with one shot from his single-barrelled twelve bore in the winter of 1939-40. And that is almost a record.

That was Mersea in the mellow days between the two wars and in the triumphant aftermath of the last war. Today, alas, Mrs. Hone and Admiral Wyatt are both dead. They lie within the sound of the bells of the little Roman church overlooking the sea. Bob South survives, wind grizzled. The Club, as such, is no more. A restaurant with a London touch has taken its place and we older ones have taken wing. Much of the old Mersea has been destroyed by the ruthless, soleless greed of speculative builders. Bungalows cluster like swarms of wood lice. In summer the coast road is pandemonium. Yachts and boats, many which seldom put to sea, litter the foreshore. Urbanisation is the enemy of this ancient isle.

Perhaps one day common sense will return and those who build houses will build them to rhyme with the surroundings. Until then, Mersea for me merely means a pilgrimage to the foreshore Oyster Bar of Douglas Mussett, one of the oldest island families. The Mussets are fishermen of renown, yacht skippers of fame and above all, owners and purveyors of Mersea oysters, the best in England. That stall on the coast road, where the gulls wheel and Jackie, the pet jackdaw, sits on your shoulder, is unique. I know no better oyster bar in all England. They come straight from the sea, down your gullet, and under their beneficence, if you shut your eyes, the inshore bungalows fade away. The old Mersea magic still lingers on the coast road where brash modern buildings, thanks to the wise will of a dead and gone Lord of the Manor, are banned.

One of Mrs. Hone's two junoesque daughters, Diana, still dwells in the village. You will find her with the wise islanders in the Fountain Inn which still holds the old spell. The spirit of Emily Hone is not dead.

The beauty of the Crouch

*Where the Lord of the Manor is Lord of the Sea . . .
a unique survival . . . town of oysters, yachts and
smugglers.*

The other day I sailed up the River Crouch. A bright day of winter sunshine when the "butterfly sailors" of summer were all safely crouched over the television or reddening their countenances in over-heated houses. The Crouch is a river of ancient history and largely of unspoiled beauty. We in Essex take such things for granted.

Why not sail up this river of old magic one weekend or motor along the valley, stop, get out and stare. If you sail up the Crouch in a boat, you will see a river, broad and shining, a river rimmed by a narrow strip of glistening mud flats. And beyond the mud flats, the green scarp of sea-walls faced with stone or with black slimy piles at the bottom, and clad for the rest in long coarse grass. In summer, if you peer over those sea-walls you will see a belt of flat and tussocky cattle-marsh which swims away in uneven waves until it breaks in a white foam of cow-parsley and hawthorn against the hedges which guard upland fields that swell to a low skyline. Dykes, brassy with kingcups, their brown water disturbed by quirking moorhens and sudden somersaults of dabchicks, cross the marshes like silver swords.

Once you have sailed beyond the wide, wild prairie of Wallasea on the south side and that great far-reaching land of flat fields of corn and grass which goes marching on mile after mile into the endless horizon of the Dengie Hundred to the north, you sail into a land of narrower marshes, lesser horizons. For this River Crouch has none of the width, the nobility, or the great skyscapes of the Blackwater. It is a long, narrow, salt river running through a shallow valley, a valley almost empty of great woods but beautified by the few remaining clumps and marching lines of those mighty hedge-row elms which were the glory of the Essex countryside until disease smote them.

Once upon a time the Crouch was a river of unblemished beauty. A man might look at the generous warmth of old red buildings ashore at Burnham, at Queen Anne facades and Georgian frontages, at a jumble of weatherboarded cottages and tarred boat-sheds, and see little inns whose windows winked most coquettishly through wisteria, and he might feel that there he saw a typical, though a humble and unpretentious, vista of English loveliness.

But today all that warm water frontage of Burnham, that marching jumble of eave and roof-tree and dormer is overshadowed and cast down in countenance. For at the eastern

Old oyster beds at Paglesham

end of this once beautiful waterfront, they have reared a monstrous grey and glittering erection of concrete and plate-glass. It lowers at the water with an uncouth superciliousness. An architectural lout let loose on the landscape.

If you sail further up the Crouch you encounter an equally regrettable but less pretentious form of slumdom. For a veritable psoriasis of bungalows and shacks, jerrybuilt, tawdry, and bumped willy-nilly, is reaching down to the shores of the upper river like a red rash. Some of these sprawling eruptions represent the worst type of private enterprise in building. We may thank the speculators who father such "developments" for most of the reasons why today the Town and Country Planning Act has clamped us into a veritable straitjacket of rules and regulations.

Fortunately not all the Crouch is yet spoilt. You may sail below the red Elizabethan walls of Creeksea Place and meditate upon this countryside as it was when the Mildmays held their Courts Baron there, for they owned much land here, even the very river itself. Over at Rochford in that still gracious hall which is now a golf club, dwelt Anne Boleyn.

It was at Rochford that they kept up that whimsical custom known as the Lawless Courts. There is nothing like it elsewhere in England. It was said of it that:

A small weatherboarded inn, the Sail and Plough at Paglesham

104

"It is kept at King's-hill—about half a mile north-east of this church—in the yard of a house once belonging to —. Cripps, Gent., and afterwards to Robt. Hackshaw, of London, merchant; and to Mr. John Buckle. Here the tenants kneel, and do their homage. The time is, the Wednesday morning next after Michaelmas-day, upon the first cock-crowing, without any kind of light, but such as the heavens will afford. The Steward of the Court calleth such as are bound to appear, with as low a voice as possible, giving no notice when he goeth to execute his office; howsoever, he that gives not an answer is deeply amerced. They are all to whisper to each other. Nor have they any pen and ink, but supply that office with a coal; and he that owes suit and service thereto, and appears not, forfeits to the Lord double his rent every hour he is absent. A tenant of this maner forfeited, not long ago, his land, for non-attendance; but was restored to it, the Lord only taking a fine. The Court is called lawless, because held at an unlawful or lawless hour, or quia dicta sine lege. The title of it runs in the Court-rolls to this day . . . . There is a tradition that this servile attendance was imposed at first upon certain tenants of divers maners hereabouts, for conspiring in this place, at such an unseasonable time, to raise a commotion. This Court belongs to Robert Bristow, Esq."

There is a drowned island in the Crouch called Bridge Marsh. When I first knew it in the "thirties" it was walled and embanked, alive with cattle, its dykes and fleets the home of a vast number of eels and of wild duck which came in hundreds. At the west end stood an old cottage, ruined and empty. And in the chimney of that cottage a pair of pereggrine falcons nested.

Then one day of easterly gales and high tides, the sea-wall broke down, the sea rushed in, and all the isle went back to the suck and eddy of tides. That day sheep were drowned in scores.

Today at high water you will see little more than the broken, ragged line of the sea-wall, a wall that is washed away foot by foot as each tide ebbs and flows. At low water the island emerges, a slimy, sodden morass of saltings and mud, home of feeding curlew and scuttling crabs. Bits of the old cottage still stand.

Half a million pounds and half-a-million oysters lie smugly invested in the River Crouch. They represent the revival of an ancient Essex industry. The half-a-million in cash represents the estimated value of the manorial rights in the oyster fisheries and other fisheries of the Crouch, which

The tall brick tower of Rochford Church silhouetted against a cloudless sky

were granted under a Royal Charter in the thirteenth century before Magna Carta was signed. Those rights, which extend from the Rays'n Channel three or four miles out to sea—where they include the Ray Sand and the Buxey Sand—right up the river to the old smugglers' haunt of Brandy Hole Creek, are almost unique in England.

I know of only one other tidal river whose fishery rights are vested in the Lord of the Manor by Royal Charter. That is the Beaulieu River in Hampshire, owned by Lord Montagu of Beaulieu. The rights in the Crouch were held for generations by the Mildmay family of Creeksea Place, who also owned land in and about Chelmsford, gave their name to a street, and made their marks in history.

The oyster fisheries of the Crouch and the River Roach have, within my lifetime, been held by Smith Brothers of Burnham and Colonel Nicholls of The Chase, Paglesham. I believe the Sweeting family, famous for their fish restaurant in the City, had a hand in them at one time.

Recently the rights have been bought by the new Burnham River Company. The result has been a new infusion of money, brains, modern methods—plus a new breed of oysters into the Burnham River.

The Great Tide of 1952/3 and the barbarously cold frosts of 1963 killed millions of oysters in the river. They virtually killed the trade altogether. The oyster fleet, which one remembers as more than twenty sail, has dwindled to two dredgers, "Sea Pie" and "Burnham Osprey". "Sea Pie" is skippered and crewed by Dick Wood, who knows more about oysters than most people. He has the wisdom of salt tides and the ancient river, the philosophy of a true countryman, and the seeing eye of a devoted naturalist. Dick saw the industry fall on hard times.

The Royal Burnham natives—and don't forget the Royal—fatten prodigiously in this Essex river of history. Roman emperors adored them a thousand years ago. They, like the Mersea oysters, were sent, packed in snow, from Burnham River to the Courts of the Caesars in Rome.

The market for them in Britain is insatiable. So is the market on the continent. "The Continent of Europe thinks so highly of Royal Burnham natives that they would probably absorb twenty times the number of oysters that this river is likely to produce", Mr. Dennis Key, Senior Scientific Officer at the Government Marine Research Station in Burnham told me.

So on September 1, a day of sunlit peace and salt spray, not only the Feast of St. Partridge but also the Feast of the Oyster, there we were, dropping the dredge overboard with a plop and hoping for a good haul. It was. There were seven of us aboard—the Earl of Denbigh and his cousin; Mr. John Meade; Mr. Phil Herring (President of the Royal Burnham Yacht Club who has done more than any man to preserve those lovely eighteenth century houses on the waterfront); David Duffy, Dick Woods, and myself. Standing in the waist of the ship, the champagne glinted in the sun as tall Rhemish glasses were filled and lifted. "To Burnham River and the Royal Burnham oyster!" A pretty little ceremony of sun and sea and winking wine.

On one side Foulness Island, flat, lonely and indepen-

The High Street on Burnham-on-Crouch. Sailing enthusiasts from all over the world visit the town to attend the annual regatta

dent. On the other Wallasea Island, where we used to round up the sheep and cattle on horseback when dear old Will Goodchild farmed those lonely acres. And ahead, Potton Island, my youthful paradise. Smugglers' country.

These creeks saw the smuggling vessels of "Hardapple" Blyth of Paglesham put to sea. Their sea silence throbbed to the far-off thunder of Blyth's brass cannon as he fought the Revenue cutter. He was not only King of the Smugglers but churchwarden at Paglesham church, keeper of a village shop, and a mighty cricketer. He wrapped up his tea and sugar in the Parish register, chewed glass for fun. When a bull charged the Paglesham cricket team, Blyth seized it by the tail, hammered it with a great club, and, hanging on, was towed by the bull off the cricket pitch, over the hedge and into the next field. They say the bull died of heart failure, but Blyth survived to a ripe old age, and on his deathbed asked for a chapter of the Bible to be read to him. Then he murmured, "Dear Lord, I am ready for the launch" and, turning his face to the wall, he died.

They say that Blyth gained his strength and valour from the fact that he swallowed Burnham oysters by the bushelful. Well, I had my dozen or two aboard "Sea Pie" and then, with a prayer for Blyth's soul, went ashore.

Essex — dustbin of London

Planners who murder our villages . . . faceless horrors of architecture . . . how they kill the village spirit and the battle to survive . . . Essex towns and villages of beauty . . . places to see from Epping to the Suffolk Stour.

Essex is becoming the dustbin of London. There are plans to extend the new towns of Harlow and Basildon. Such plans should be fought. Let us hope that the opposition will be vigorous, well-documented and tough. It is high time that the wholesale spoilation of the rich farmlands of Essex by speculative builders and others is brought to a halt.

The proposed Third London Airport at Willingale is in the news. It is an outstanding example of the way in which this richly fertile county, still in parts, of singular unspoilt beauty, is being gradually robbed of its agricultural values and brutalised into ugliness. We are making gods of machines at the expense of human values.

So-called "planners" in Government departments who, apparently, look at a blank space on the map and say "Ah! Splendid place for a New Town or a Third London Airport" are largely to blame. One wonders if any of them have any practical knowledge of rural values, particularly farming values.

Too many private speculators who build without any regard to the traditional architectural values of the countryside, are also to blame. They blister our rural beauty by building endless acres of featureless bungalows, jerry-built houses—all breeze-blocks, glass and formica—and leave the wretched owners to pay the mortgage and wait for the cracks to appear in the walls. Fortunately the clamp down on building and the sharper inquiry into costings will deter some of these get-rich-quick jerry-builders.

Meanwhile, let us fight to preserve the architectural beauty which is the singular and gracious heritage of so many Essex towns and villages.

We must preserve what we have and make the most of it. Many an old house or row of cottages can be modernised at little cost and thus trebled in value. People pay willingly for beauty and tradition.

Essex is full of lovely old towns and delectable villages. Its countryside is a continuous pageant of history. It has been the front battle-line of England since the first Vikings in their dragon-headed ships sailed up our rivers, shield-hung, with that blood-chilling war-cry of "Yuch! Hey! Saa-saa" going before them on the wind. Norseman, Dane, Dutchman, Frenchman and German, have all assaulted our beaches,

A Sunday afternoon walk in Epping forest in summer

sent up our towns in flames, slain our forbears—and been repulsed bloodily.

Today the enemy is from within. Our ancient towns and lovely villages are being destroyed, disfigured, raped and cheapened not by foreign enemies, but by speculative builders, bird-cage architects and the apostles of "Get-rich-quick-at-any-price".

Brentwood, once a charming old country town, is now a cheap-jack appanage of suburban London. The old centre of Chelmsford has been pulled down to make way for "modern development". The result is a hideous girdle of modern horrors which have completely destroyed most of the old charm and beauty of the town. There was little enough of that in any case.

In Cambridge the appalling excrescences of Churchill College - the sight of which, one hears, made Winston spit with fury - and the brash ugliness of the Keynes building in Kings - and other concrete-and-glass horrors, including that highly dispensable erection by the late Sir Basil Spence in the gardens of Queen's are barely offset by the enlightened good architecture of some of the extensions to John's and other colleges.

Most of those who live in north-west Essex regard Cambridge not only as by far their best and nearest big-scale shopping centre, but also as a place to which they can take friends for a day's sight seeing among some of the best architecture in Europe. It is a city of unique and haunting beauty. There is only one King's College Chapel in the world. There is nothing elsewhere in England to match the riverside beauty of the Backs. The Victorians, who were pretty good at destroying old houses and replacing them with hideous erections of white Cambridge brick and drab Welsh slate which grow uglier with time, luckily built most of their excrescences on the fringe of the town. The Newmarket Road area is the best example of this sort of thing.

Today the modern architects, including the late Sir Basil Spence, have gate-crashed the academic centre of the City and put up new buildings and colleges which seem as though they were designed deliberately to cock a snoop at the immemorial beauty of King's, Trinity Great Court, Queen's, Peterhouse and other gems. A classic example of unforgivable ugliness is the new wing of John's built like a multi-storey glass garage on the banks of the river. The restoration conversion of an old street block nearby, done with exquisite taste, emphasises what can be done with old buildings. It is a masterpiece.

One could multiply the dreary tale of destruction on the

fringes of village after village in Essex. The worst of all modern horrors is the new town of Haverhill on the borderline of Essex and Suffolk. It is unbelievable. One wonders how any mother could bring up a family of small children in such brutalisingly ugly surroundings and expect them to grow into normal citizens with a love of that simple beauty of old village architecture which so many Essex villages possess.

Fortunately west and north-west Essex still preserve such old towns and villages as Saffron Walden, Thaxted, parts of Bishop's Stortford and Dunmow, Hallingbury, Coggeshall - the old silk weaving town—most of Witham and Kelvedon, most of Epping, Ongar - which still has the atmosphere of a country town although you can reach it from Central London by underground railway - Blackmore, Writtle, and, of course, that bevy of villages in the Rodings which take their names from the River Roding. God has looked on the Rodings with a benevolent eye. It is a land of rich and heavy

Springtime in Epping forest

soil which makes small fortunes for farmers. It is foggy in winter and its winding lanes keep the average motorist more or less at bay. Only the discerning go to Good Easter, High Easter, Magdalen Laver, White Roding, Leaden Roding, Margaret Roding, High Roding and the hilariously named Shellow Bowels which seems to suggest permanent gastric disorder. All have simple charm, architectural beauty and an air of independence. They have not yet been swamped by undesirable villas of dubious construction which the builders elsewhere proclaim as firm to stand for ten years - no more. Heaven help the young people who pin their mortgage futures to such erections.

Few counties have lovelier villages than Essex. Not merely the picture postcard villages of the Suffolk border such as Dedham, Lavenham and Kersey, but the less well-known towns and villages such as Braintree, Bocking, Halstead - with its particular charm, Great Easton, Broxted, Bures, Felsted, and that salt water little port Manningtree—full of sea gulls and little ships. All these have preserved much of their atmosphere of the past. They should be jealously guarded. Maldon, with its active Maldon Society, gives the lead in this constant war against ugliness and builders' greed.

The little town which best preserves the true feudal atmosphere is Castle Hedingham. There is nothing else in England quite like it. And there was no mightier castle in East Anglia. It was built probably about 1140 and belonged for more than 600 years to the de Veres, Earls of Oxford. Aubrey de Vere, son of the Aubrey who came with the Conqueror to England in 1066, built the castle of which this is the tower keep, in the reign of King Stephen, when the Barons maintained private armies and England was racked by their wars.

There were seventeen Earls of Oxford. John de Vere took his private army to fight for Henry VII at Bosworth Field. He was almost as powerful as the King himself with vast estates in Essex and elsewhere. Years later he invited King Henry to Castle Hedingham. There he entertained his monarch with such military pomp, splendour of pageantry and such richness of food and wine, that he broke all the laws laid down to curb baronial power. He entertained the King as though he were a king himself. The King promptly fined his host £10,000 - probably equal to a million today - for his daring.

Today Castle Hedingham village is still a medieval village in looks, spirit and atmosphere. Come to it in the glory of a setting sun, the mystery of dusk, and the narrow streets and old houses seem alive with the men and women of the heroic past. Here is a place where time stands still but no dust gathers.

Nearly every Essex village has its manor house, great or small. Usually they were the homes of squires who farmed most of their own land, held their manorial courts at which they administered justice. They were the friends and guardians of their tenants. It was a very close to earth, friendly set-up. The best of the Roding manor houses to my mind is that superb brick and timber moated house, Colville Hall at White Roding.

Canvey ~ island of history

*Seething surburban satellite of London . . . ghosts
. . . invaders . . . and modern menace.*

Not long ago, the Government set up a Health and Safety Executive to look at the dangers to Canvey Island, and to neighbouring Thurrock, of the concentration of oil and chemical storage and processing installations. In July, 1978, the Health and Safety Executive reported that if certain improvements were made they would be satisfied that there was no additional risk in the construction of further chemical oil installations on the island. Local authorities are challenging this. One of them, the Castle Point District Council, which represents Benfleet and Canvey, bluntly demands that the existing British Gas Methane terminal should be closed down. Good luck to them. I hope they win. Canvey and Benfleet were old when Southend was an infant. They defied Roman, Dane and Dutchman. Today, Canvey, and the old Benfleet town defy the Moloch of so-called "progress." You will remember that the Moloch was a Canaanite idol that devoured small children.

Canvey Island is now linked to the mainland by a high-level road bridge under which boats can sail. The population has grown from a few hundreds when I first knew it in the 1920s, to many thousands. The old bridge, which was opened in 1931 and stood for just over forty years, knew the urgent traffic of guns, tanks and men in the last war. It knew also the tragic traffic of the drowned-out, homeless thousands of Canvey people who, in the Great Flood of 1953, came across it, cold, sodden and miserable, to warmth and shelter in Benfleet and beyond.

Today, Canvey is a great seething surburban satellite of London. Good roads, good shops, streets of houses and neat bungalows, neon lights, cinemas and bingo. You might as well be in Putney, were it not for the sea wall, the strong smell of salt tides and the strident fog horns.

Odd to think that a few years before the bridge was opened in 1924, I got off the midnight train at Benfleet and stumbled in the starlit dark down to the shore where the bridge now stands. I wore thigh boots, a rough shooting jacket and carried a great double barrelled duck gun, a cartridge bag and a mackintosh.

A rowing boat rocked in the little waves on the muddy foreshore. I climbed aboard. Three or four island men and women grunted brief greetings. The ferryman pushed off. He dipped his oars, pulled, and the beamy old boat butted her bows into the tide. Waves slapped the side and sprayed up with salt. On the far shore a dim light glimmered. That was

Southend can be seen through the mist at dusk as these fishermen on Canvey Island wait patiently for a bite

117

the only sign of life.

After a few minutes' rowing the boat grounded by a rough "hard" of flat stones. If you got out carefully and trod like a cat you could, with luck, avoid shipping a couple of bootfuls.

In the half light on the shingly track which passed for a road, the island motor bus waited. It was, to be precise, an old Ford van set on the high wheels with enormous clearance of the original Tin Lizzie type. The back doors had no glass. They were wide open to the wind but covered in chicken wire. It had a dual purpose. First, to blow out the petrol fumes which almost choked the passengers inside — you were forbidden on pain of death to smoke aboard the bus. Second, as the bus rolled and bucked like a bronco over the potholes of the island roads, the chicken net made sure the passengers were not chucked out.

As I stepped ashore from that aged rowing boat which was the only "official" communication with the mainland, a little man with gold ear-rings in his ears, wind-bitten face, sharp eyes and a bush of hair looked at me hard and said: "Are you Mr. Wentworth Day?" I admitted the offence.

"Come yew along o'me", he said and hauled me into the bus. Never before or since have I seen a man with such a piratical cut to his jib. He might have stepped straight out of the reign of Queen Elizabeth I and have walked ashore an hour before at the nearby Lobster Smack from one of Drake or Grenville's privateers.

That was Charlie Stamp, of Canvey Point, professional wildfowler, inshore fisherman and general beachcomber. I had answered an advertisement in the *Shooting Times,* offering to provide rough wildfowling at weekends. "Rough" was the operative word. Charlie could neither read nor write, so he got a neighbour to indite a postcard saying he would meet me at the ferryboat that night.

Charlie lived in a little wooden house built from the salvaged timbers of an old sailing barge, right under the sea wall at Canvey Point. He had built it himself. It was about two up and two down and you went up a wooden ladder to the attic where I slept.

Charlie believed in ghosts and witches; and he spoke with proper respect of Cunning Murrell, the wise man or wizard who had lived in an old cottage with his books and spells, his potions and medieval chemistry, his curses and warnings under the shadow of Hadleigh Castle ruins.

There were a few bungalows on Canvey in those days. A few rather tawdry shops. Made-up roads glittered with puddles. In summer Londoners came down in shoals and slept or camped whereever they could find accommodation. The westward end of the island was still flat grass marshes, seamed with dykes. A few big old blackboarded farmhouses stood up like ships in the lonely plain.

The Lobster Smack, old as time, with a wavy roof which hid three centuries of smuggling secrets and deeds of piracy, huddled under the sea wall at the mouth of Holehaven Creek, Charles Dickens loved it and put it in Great Expectations. You could step out of the bedroom window on to a plank and walk straight on to the top of the sea wall. It was kept by Jimmy Went, whose family had been in Essex for three or four hundred years. From his I first learnt the legend of the Dragon of Herongate, which came out of Bulphan Fen, ravaged the countryside, slew cattle, devoured babies, scared women out of their wits and sent Sir John Tyrrell, of Heron Hall, forth, sword in hand, to slay it in the wild wood which

A pastoral scene on Canvey Island. In the distance the chimneys of the oil refineries on the island

they still call Picketts (or Picot's) Bushes at the back of East Horndon Church.

He beheaded the dragon and took the ghastly head, dripping with blood, to show his wife who was about to bear child. She screamed in fright, collapsed and died weeks later. Sir John strode back in a fury to the Bushes and, livid with sorrow and rage, kicked the rotting corpse of the dragon. A poisoned bone pierced his foot. He was dead within weeks.

Be that as it may, when Claudius Ptolemy, the Roman geographer who flourished in the reign of Hadrian, was drawing his maps just over 1,900 years ago, he mapped Canvey as an island and named it Cnossos. So you see Canvey has a long, long history. In Roman days it was no more than a great sodden sea marsh.

Then Joas van Cropenbrugh, the Dutch drainer, was hired by Sir Henry Appleton, the Essex Wentworths and other landowners on April 9, 1622, to embank Canvey. He shut out the sea. The round Dutch houses, the treasured antiquarian relics of the island today, are the visible reminders of the Dutch "occupation".

The Dutch came back again in the reign of Charles II, when Van Tromp sailed his fleet up the Thames and lobbed a cannon-ball or two into more than one Thames-side village. They landed a party of baggy-breeched Dutch sailors, who rounded up a few score island sheep, cut their throats and took them aboard to victual their ships.

Long before that Hasten, the Danish sea king, laid up his grim fleet of sea-serpents or long-ships in Benfleet Creek, where at low water they were burnt out by Saxons, presumably, led by Charlie Stamp's fiftieth great-grandfather.

My memory of Canvey in the last war was of an inspiring night with an ack-ack battery on the island, when night after night the German raiders came over like flights of nightmare wildfowl.

Imagine yourself for a moment in the concrete firing room where tin-hatted youngsters, brown as berries, serious eyed, listened intently at telephones, pore over the plotting table. Staccato words and phrases are rapped out. Somewhere out in the moon haze a great black Ju 88, loaded with sea mines, swoops low over the estuary like a ghastly nighthawk.

"Fire!" Tongues of flame sear the half-light, the reports thud through the riven silence. A mile out over the dark water the shells burst, red and yellow flowers in the night.

Other reports thud forth, other shells whine out and burst. The black nighthawk, caught in a withering blast of splinter and concussion, lurches. A shell strikes fair and square; its mine load explodes with a shattering detonation.

Bits and pieces of fuselage, wings, struts, and men rain down into the water.

Charlie Stamp capped that lot in World War One. A Zeppelin, hard hit by London gunfire, came limping down the Thames on its way home to Germany. It was barely a hundred yards up. Charlie, crouching in a rill in the saltings waiting for the evening duck flight, upped with his great double-barrelled eight-bore and let drive four ounces of swan-shot "as big as doctors' pills" at the Germans in the cabin slung beneath the vast bulk of the airship.

Next morning an irate officer from Southend arrived at Charlie's house and blew him up in no uncertain fashion for having taken the war into his own hands: "You might have made that airship drop the last of its bombs on Southend."

"They tell me that owd Zepp, come down in the North Sea", Charlie retorted. "If that did, I reckon I done it. You didn't! Goo you back to the Army and learn to shoot."

I wonder if those who live in the bungalows of modern Canvey ever see the ghost of the Viking who, one moonlight night, splashed ashore through the shallow tide on Canvey Point, walked over the sea wall and across the dyke into Charlie's bedroom. Charlie told me the story.

"I laid in me truckle bed and saw the man come out of the water, over the sea wall and in at me bedroom window. He stood by the bed, dripping with salt water and looked at me right sorrowful, 'What do you want mate?' I asked. 'Who are ye.' 'I've lost me ship, lost me mates and lost me way,' he said. 'I want to get home to Denmark.'

" 'Go ye up river,' I said, 'to Gray's or Tilbury and you'll get a ship to any port in the world.' That old boy looked at me right sorrowful. He wore a leather jerkin, what looked like strapped gaiters up to his knees, and a steel helmet with wings standing out over his ears. He carried a short sword in his belt and a battle axe in his hand. He was a Viking, sure as fate. I have seen 'em in coloured pictures.

" 'You don't understand' he said in a sorrowful voice. 'Me ship was sunk here in the creek outside and me mates were all killed by you Saxons. Now I am left alone and I can't get home.' He turned round, went out of the winder, along the plank which leads from the winder to the top of the sea wall, and then on the saltings and the mud flats. He made for the sea and splashed into it. He turned once and waved farewell to me, sad and sorrowful-like. Then the water swallowed him up. I ain't never seen him since".

That is the true tale of the sad ghost of Canvey Island.

The Wentworths of Essex

The late Sir Bernard Burke wrote a book at the end of the last century entitled *Vicissitudes of Families*. In it he traced the noblemen and landed gentry who from bearing ancient titles and having great estates had sunk to penury or complete obscurity. It is a sad, fascinating record, largely confined to Irish families. Had he extended his researches into Essex and East Anglia, he would have included the Wentworths of Nettlestead, Suffolk, Codham Hall, Essex, Gosfield Hall, Essex, and their off-shoots at Lillingstone Lovell in Buckinghamshire from whom we descend through the marriage in 1563 of William Day, eldest son of Dr. William Day 12th Provost of Eton, Dean of the Chapel Royal of Windsor and Bishop of Winchester, to Helen, daughter of Paul Wentworth, M.P., of Burnham Abbey, Buckinghamshire.

I am lucky enough to have inherited from the late Baroness Wentworth of Nettlestead and Crabbet Park, Sussex, the complete pedigree of these three branches of the Wentworth family with their Berkshire and Buckinghamshire offshoots.

Let us consider the power, prestige and lands of this once great family in Essex. When Sir John Wentworth entertained Elizabeth I at Gosfield, he owned no less than sixty-one manors in Essex, Suffolk and Norfolk, about 50,000 acres. Forty-one of those manors were in Essex. Today I doubt if any Wentworths own more than an acre or two in any of these three counties with the exception of Blackheath estate of more than 4,000 acres near Aldburgh.

The Wentworth manors in Essex, greatly augmented by marriages with heiresses of the Helion, Howard, FitzSimon, Tyrrell and Darcy families, were the following:

Harmours (Monthermers), Parkehall, Hodinges als. Churchehall, Bellhouse, Sharlowes (Shardlowes), Aylewardes were in the immediate vicinity of Gosfield. Going northward towards the border of the county: Syble-Hynyngham als. Syble-Heddingham, Maplested Magna, Maplested.

Overhall in Gestlingthorpe, Bulmer, Otten-Belcham, Belcham-Williams als. Walter-Belcham, Pawles-Belcham, Borley, Foxerthe, Lyston, Pentlowe, Ovington, Ashen. Eastward of Gosfield were Hawstide (Halstead?), Bewers (Bures), Withermoundeforde (Wormingford), Garner als. Garnon, Magna Horksley.

Horkesley, St. Marie (?), Fordam. Westward of Gosfield were Wethersfield, Coddham oulde pke. et Coddham newe pke., Shalforde, Shornhall (Sherne Hall), Nicholls, Fynchingefelde, Nortofts, Magna Bardefilde, Pva. Bardfelde. Southward were Bovington, Bockynge, Pva. Reyne, Brantree (Braintree). To this list may be added from Morant's account, Liston Hall, Biggs (now Gosfield Place) and Morells, near Gosfield; Barkers or Bakers in Wethersfield; Cornett or Cornish Hall in Finchingfield; Bumpstead-Helion; Cheswick Hall in Chrishall; East Mersea exchanged for Wethersfield, with lands and a town house (now shops) in Maldon.

I give their original spelling, a medieval cadence of Essex place names.

The three branches of the family which descended from the parent stock in Yorkshire, produced one barony (that of Wentworth of Nettlestead), nine Knights, three Sheriffs of Norfolk and Suffolk, two Sheriffs of Essex and Hertfordshire, several Royal envoys and Knights of the Shire who were distinguished Parliamentarians. More than one Lord Wentworth was imprisoned. Sir Philip Wentworth (Nettlestead) who fought as a Lancastrian in the War of the Roses was captured at the Battle of Hexham in 1464 and beheaded.

The 1st Lord Wentworth founded the Coldstream Guards. The 2nd Baron, Sir Thomas, fought at the Battle of Pinkie in 1547 and was later made the last English Governor of Calais.

He complained bitterly to Queen Mary of its defencelessness before the French captured it. He was taken prisoner, ransomed, returned home, tried for high treason in the House of Lords and unanimously acquitted. The 3rd Baron led a blameless, quiet life. The 4th was a fighting man and a Parliamentarian. He fought for the Stuart cause in the Civil war and was ruined. He was a close friend of his relative, Thomas Wentworth, the "Great Earl" of Strafford, Lord President of the Council of the North and Lord Deputy of Ireland, the strong man of Charles I's reign, whose advice, had it been taken, might have averted the Civil War. Thomas Lord Wentworth was present at Strafford's trial and execution. I own one of the three existing copies of Strafford's last speech on the scaffold, as well as several copies of his State papers, a large, leather-bound account of his "Tyral", his school books, annotated in his own hand, and a handsome gilt and leather-bound copy of Virgil which Strafford read during his imprisonment in the Tower. These came to me from Wentworth Castle near Barnsley and from Wentworth Woodhouse, near Rotherham, together with many pictures and furniture of the Stuart period.

But to get back to Gosfield, Queen Elizabeth I paid a highly expensive and majestically staged visit there where she was entertained by Sir John Wentworth in 1561. She arrived from Helmingham Hall, that lovely moated place in Suffolk where the Tollemaches lived and still live. The family records state that "she arrived on 19 August and remained at Gosfield until the 21st when she went on to Leighs to visit Lord Rich . . .".We here find the expenses daily entered under the heads, "Pantry, Buttery, Wardrobe, Kitchen, Poultry, Scullery, Salt-Moats, Hall and Chamber, Stable, Vails or Presents, and Charity". And the totals at Gosfield were for 19 August £107/9s. 11¾d. and for 20 August £104/12s. 11d." One shudders at the price equivalent today.

In 1566, the year before he died, Sir John Wentworth was given the custody at Gosfield of an illustrious State prisoner, Lady Katharine Grey, cousin of Queen Elizabeth and sister of poor Lady Jane Grey, the ten days' Queen. She had previously been in the charge of Mr. Secretary Petre (later Lord Petre) at Ingatestone Hall where her initials are pathetically scratched on the chimney piece in her room. After Sir John's death, Lady Katharine was sent to Sir Owen Hopton's house at Yoxford in Suffolk, where she died soon after. Lady Katharine was just twenty-seven years old when she died and her only sin had been to marry the Earl of Hertford without the Queen's consent.

Sir John had recently built the house at Gosfield in Elizabethan style on a grand scale, his forebears having moved from Nettlestead to Codham Hall near Shalford in Essex, now occupied by the Tabor family.

Queen Elizabeth appreciated her stay at Gosfield so much that she returned there for five days in August 1597 after Sir John's death when his daughter, Lady Maltravers, was her hostess.

During Elizabeth's reign, Sir Peter Wentworth, M.P. of Lillingstone Lovell, "the unconquerable Sir Peter" as Hallam called him, played a prominent part in the Queen's affairs. In an era when Parliament was the pawn of the Sovereign and most of its Members terrified of the Queen, he was sent three times to the Tower for his outspoken defence of Parliamentary rights. The third time was at the age of seventy when he had urged the sixty-year old Queen to nominate her successor. She was livid. Wentworth and his wife, Elizabeth Walsingham, both remained in the Tower for the rest of their lives. Both died there.

The last of the Wentworths of Gosfield and Codham was a fool. That is the kindest word one can apply to Sir John Wentworth, Knight, and later Baronet, born about 1583 who died in obscurity in October 1631. The manner of his death and the place of his burial are unknown. The good family record was smirched and the estates scattered by a misguided ass who came into his great fortune too early after a youth spent at the court of James I where he learned bad habits and spent money like water.

John Wentworth was knighted at the age of twenty in 1603 when James I made a triumphal progress from Edinburgh to London to ascend the throne on the death of Elizabeth I. The Scottish King was in high fettle and lavish of honours. He had a sharp eye for money as one would expect of a Scot. The chronicler of the King's progress relates that on the 22nd of April, 1603, "Sir William Pelham, High Sheriff of Lincolnshire, received his Highness (coming from Newark-on-Trent) being gallantly appointed with both horse and men, divers worshipful men of the same country accompanied him, who convoyed and guarded his Majesty to Bever (Belvoir) Castle, being the right noble Earl of Rutland's, where his Highness was not only royally and most plentifully recieved, but with such exceeding joy of the good Earl and his honourable lady that he took therein exceeding pleasure. And he approved his contentment in the morning, for before he went to break his fast he made these knights whose names follow". No less than forty-nine gentlemen were dubbed knights by happy King James before he went to breakfast, and in the list of those honoured is named 'Sir John Wentworth of Essex'.

Sir John spent the next six years travelling abroad. There he probably picked up more bad habits. In 1610 he was appointed a Gentleman of the Chamber to Henry, Prince of Wales. The following year, James I, with his Scottish respect for money, created the Order of Baronetage. Sir John Wentworth, the last of the Gosfield line, was the first Baronet in the family. The order was open to gentlemen of good birth and position with an estate of not less than £1,000 a year. In the family pedigree is this engaging entry: "they had to pay into the Exchequer a sum equivalent to three years' pay of thirty soldiers, at eightpence per day per man, nominally for service in the Province of Ulster, Ireland. The cost of a Baronetcy thus amounted to £1,095." That sum could well represent up to £100,000 in our debased currency today. The reference to the need to finance troops in Ulster also has a sardonic ring at the present time.

By that time the Gosfield estates had already begun to break up. The year before Sir John spent this large sum on his Baronetcy, an Act was passed "to enable Sir John Wentworth to sell lands for payment of his debts". The Rake's Progress was getting into its stride.

1612 saw him marching in solemn state as one of the six pall-bearers bearing aloft the canopy of black velvet under which rested the dead body of his Prince and master, Henry, Prince of Wales. More than 2,000 mourners followed the coffin in "sumptuous funeral pomp".

The family papers have little or nothing to say on his conduct over the next four years. Then came the mysterious murder in the Tower of London in 1613 of that wise and good man, Sir Thomas Overbury. Somehow, we do not know precisely how, Sir John Wentworth was involved. Two years after the murder, Robert Carr, Earl of Somerset, the revolting 'favourite" of the slobbering Scottish King, was charged with the crime. His Countess, the divorced wife of the Earl of Essex, was included in the charge. The Countess confessed her guilt. Carr was convicted and sentenced to death. James I pardoned them both within a few days. Then, on the principle that if the high and mighty are acquitted, somone else of lower degree must carry the blame, Sir Jervis Elvis, (Lieutenant of the Tower) Richard Weston, (a warder) and two other people were charged, condemned and executed. Sir John Wentworth was rash enough to interrogate Weston on the scaffold. What right he had to be there, no one knows. Nor do we know his motive. There is no hint that he took part in the murder. Like other fools, he merely rushed in where wiser men feared to tread. As a newspaper man, I have often wondered if this addle-headed forebear was not trying to be the crime reporter of his day. However, whatever his motive may have been, it cost him another £1,000. More Gosfield manors had to be sold to pay for this folly.

Then came another disaster. King James raised an expeditionary force of some 2,200 men to go to the Continent to recover the dominions of his son-in-law, Frederick the Elector Palatine. He was a Protestant, became King of Bohemia and was promptly attacked by the Catholic Kings and Princes of Germany. Among the leaders of the English force were the Earls of Oxford and Essex with 250 men each and Sir John Wentworth of Gosfield with 200 men, under the overall command of Sir Horace Vere who was almost certainly one of the de Veres of Castle Hedingham. Vere fought a brave little war for two years against overwhelmingly superior German forces. The two earls came home after six months, disillusioned with the contest. Sir John made no mark on the history of the campaign. We may perhaps regard him, if we are to be kind, as a fillibustering young man, a Gentleman Adventurer, with more bravery than brain.

Two years after his armed foray on behalf of the King of Bohemia, comes another mystery. A letter of 1622 among the State Papers, from Sir Thomas Wilson to the Earl of Salisbury, relates, with other news, that Sir John Wentworth and another are sent to gaol for murder. No explanation is given. I cannot discover who was murdered, where the murder took place, or where Sir John was imprisoned. Mr. Loftie Rutton, the family historian, says that in this year, 1622, Sir John "was compelled to vest in trustees the manor of Gosfield — Bellhouse and other manors adjacent; and in the year following 'a recovery was passed for the use of Sir John Garrard, Knight and Baronet'; in other words, the possession of the Gosfield estate passed form the Wentworths with the exception of a few manors which had probably been settled on Lady Wentworth and her daughters."

His next adventure was pure fantasy. He was commissioned by the King to go to Madrid with a dazzling present of jewels which were to be given away to the Infanta of Spain who was being courted by Prince Charles (later Charles I). The Marquess, later Duke, of Buckingham, was in charge of the Prince. But in spite of this glittering bait, the Spanish marriage did not come off. Charles married Henrietta of France. Even as a Royal matchmaker, Sir John Wentworth's luck was out.

Two years later, more or less landless and still hanging about the Court, he tried to join a second expeditionary force for the recovery of the Palatinate. The army commanders turned him down. He was cruelly cold-shouldered. The sands were running out. So he turned pirate. Privateer was the politer word.

In 1627 and the two following years he was at sea. War had broken out with France. The Government granted him the loan of a French prize ship, the Notre Dame de Grace of 160 tons, and a pinnace St. Peter, of 50 tons. He was a gentleman pirate with a fleet of two under the blessing of the State but without official recognition. He was no luckier at sea than he had been on land. He captured no French ships. Instead the French captured him. He was imprisoned at Dunkirk, but true to form, escaped. He may have been foolish but he was no coward.

Next he petitioned the King for an extended loan of his two ships which somehow or other were still in our hands. He wanted to make a voyage to the West Indies, doubtless as a pirate, then a more or less gentlemanly profession. Drake and Raleigh had set the fashion. The petition was granted but somehow things went wrong for the next thing we know was that the ships were put up for sale in July 1630. Then in the following November Sir John petitioned the King again that the £200, for which the Notre Dame had been sold be paid to him, and the vessels restored to him, he giving such satisfaction to the buyer as the Commissioners for the sale of prize ships shall think fit. The calendared State Papers, the chief source of our information, from this point are silent. Poor Sir John died in October 1631.

There is no record of how he died or where he was buried. He was only forty-eight. He was more fool than knave, more brave than wise. Had he had a good spanking as a boy, he might have made a better man!

Thus ended a branch of our family whose roots in Essex were widespread and struck deep. There were Wentworths at Mountnessing, Great and Little Horkesley, Maldon, Southend — then a hamlet — Stepney in the East End where they had a country manor house handy for London, and elsewhere. You can find their tombs in Gosfield Church and at Wethersfield.

Sir John's widow, the daughter of Sir Moyle Finch of Eastwell Park in Kent, was left a few manors to provide her with an income. She died in 1639 and is buried under the communion table in old Epping Church. There in her last years she had lived with her daughter Cecily, Lady Grey, wife of William, Lord Grey of Werke, who had purchased Epping manor from his wife's uncle, Thomas Finch, Earl of Winchilsea.

By coincidence, I took a lease of the manor house of Epping Place which incorporates old Winchilsea House, during the last war and our daughter, Clare, was baptized in the church where the tragic widow of the last Sir John

Wentworth lies buried.

After the Wentworths, Gosfield passed by a "recovery" to Sir John Garrard and by sale or marriage to Lord Colerance; Thomas Allen of Finchley, Middlesex; Francis, Lord Dacre, who sold them to Thomas Grey, son of Lord Grey. Thomas Grey left the estates to his father, Lord Grey, who had married Anne, daughter of Sir John Wentworth. Thus happily for thirty-seven years (1654-1691) the place was again in Wentworth hands on the female side.

Then it was acquired by Sir Thomas Millington, Knight, President of the College of Physicians, who lies in the Wentworth chapel at Gosfield. The Millingtons sold the Hall to Sir John Knight, M.P. who rebuilt the north, south and eastern fronts. His widow married Earl Nugent, who made the splendid lake, nearly a mile long — the largest private lake in Essex. In 1788 the Hall passed to Nugent's daughter, the Marchioness of Buckingham.

Louis XVIII, the exiled King of France, lived there form 1807-14, presumably as the Buckingham's tenant. Then in 1854 Samuel Courtauld bought it with what remained of the once-vast estates and left it to his adopted daughter, a Mrs. Lowe. Her son, Commander Lowe still owns the remnants of the property.

Today Gosfield is still a secluded and unspoiled corner of rural Essex. There have been plans to build on it in a suburban sort of fashion and some houses have arisen which are quite out of place in the country. There was talk recently of a scheme to sell so-called "leisure plots" of a quarter of an acre each for about £1,000 each. This provoked widespread opposition not only from local councils but from people much further afield who are determined that this part of England shall remain English and not merely a blot on the landscape of "litter plots" in the hands of God-knows who. I am sure that the Gosfield Parish Council and the Braintree District Council will keep a watchful eye on any future developments. Gosfield is too good to be vulgarised.

INDEX

(Folios in italic type indicate photographs)

Abberton Reservoir – *34, 37,* 39
Abdy (Sir William) – 61
Alfred the Great – 97
Allen (Thomas) – 129
Anlaf the Dane – 7
Anne (Queen) – 103
Appleton (Sir Henry) – 120
Ashingdon – 17, *18, 19*
Assandun – 16
Athenaeum – 56
Audley End – 78, *88,* 88, 92, 95
Audley (Thomas) – 93
Aveley – 78

Bailey's – 83
Baring-Gould (Rev. S.) – 98
Barrett-Lennard – 78, 81
Basildon – 111
Bassett (Sir Edward) – 78
Battlesbridge – 16
Beaulieu River – 106
Beeleigh Abbey – 7, *8,* 9, 13
Beeton (Mrs.) – 99, 100
Bell House – 77, 78, 81
Benfleet – 117, 120
Billericay – 84
Bishop's Stortford – 113
Blackmore Highwoods – 84, 113
Blackwater – 7, 61, 62, 70, 74, *74,* 103
Blyth ('Hardapple') – 109
Boadicea – 47, 50
Bocking – 114
Boleyn (Anne) – 104
Boreham – 45
Bosworth Field – 114
Bowcher (Fred) – 55
Boyard – 69
Bradwell – 7, *24, 26,* 27, 28, 29, *29, 30,* 75, 97
Braintree – 114
Brancaster – 25, 27
Brandy Hole Creek – 106
Braybrooke (Lord) – 78, 95
Braxted – 78
Brentwood – 77, 83, 84, 112
Bridges (Victor) – 99
Bright (Edward) – 7
Brightlingsea – 51
Brittany – 75
British Gas – 117
British Museum – 30
Brithnoth – 7
Broxted– 114
Buckingham (Marchioness of) – 129
Buckhurst Hill – 115
Bulphan Fen – 119
Bures – 114
Burke (Sir Bernard) – 122
Burne Jones – 115
Burnham – 103, 107, *108*
Burnham Abbey (Bucks.) – 122
Burgh Castle (Yarmouth) – 27
Burroughs (Frank) – 38
Bury St. Edmunds – 47
Buxey Sand – 106

Cambridge – 45, 48, 91, 112
Canewdon – 10, 12, *14, 16,* 16
Canterbury – 28
Canute – 12, 15, 16, 17
Canvey – 117, *117,* 118, *119,* 120, 121
Canvey Point – 65
Castle Hedingham – 77, 78, 114, 127
Castle Point – 117
Cedd (Bishop) – 28, 29
Chancellor (Wykeham) – 29
Charles I – 127
Charles II – 93
Chateau Latour – 51
Chelmsford – 40, *41,* 41, *42,* 42, *44,* 83, 84, 107, 112
Chelmsford Cathedral – 30, *43,* 43
Chelmsford Chronicle – 9
Churchill College – 112
Churchill (Sir Winston) – 100
Codham Hall – 122, 125
Coggeshall – 113
Colchester – 15, *46,* 47, 48, 50, *50,* 51, *51,* 69, 77, 78, 97, 98
Coldstream Guards – 123
Colerance (Lord) – 129
Colne Point – 38
Colville Hall – 90, 115
Constable (John) – 53, *56,* 91
Count de la Chapelle – 61, 69
Crab and Winkle Railway – 59, 60, 63
Crabbet Park, Sussex – 122
Creeksea Place – 104, 106
Cromwell – 47, 50
Cranmer-Byng (Lt. Col.) – 81
Crouch – 102, 103, 104, 105, 107
Crouch (River) – 11, 16, 17

Dacre (Lord) – 129
Dagenham – 84
Danbury – 7, 45, 78
Danegeld – 15
Day (William) – 122
Dedham – 52, 54, *54,* 55, 114
Denbigh (Earl of) – 107
Dengie Hundred – 12, *57,* 66, 103
de Veres – 79. 114, 127
D'Wit (Becky) – 75
Dickens Charles – 119
Diocletian – 25
Dover – 27, 59
Ducane (Mr.) – 78
Dunkirk – 128
Dunlin – 35, 65
Dunmow – 113
Duke of Buckingham – 127

Earls Colne – *79*
East Horndon – 120
Easton Park – 80
Eastwell Park (Kent) – 128
Elizabeth I – 9, 77, 78, 118, 123, 124, 125
Elmstead – 78
Epping – *110,* 113, *113,* 115, 128

Essex Estuary Co. – 28
Essex Folk – 12
Essex Countryside – 36, 38
Essex Union – 83, 84
Ethelred the Unready – 15, 17
Eton – 122
Evelyn (John) – 99

Fairfax (General) – 50
Feering Halt – 62
Felsted – 114
Ford Motor Co. – 86
Foulness – 11, 38, 66, 107
Foyle (Christina) – 9, 13
Frederick the Elector – 127
Flatford – *56*
Fulbridge – 7

Garrad (Sir John) – 129
Georg (Prince) – 19
Gidea Park – 31
Gimson (Dr. Carl) – 66
Goddard (Lord) – 99
Goldhanger – 73
Good Easter – 114
Goose and Dicky Railway – 59
Gosfield Hall – 122, 123, 124, 125, 126, 127, 128, 129
Grays – 121
Great Chesterford – *90*
Great Easton – 114
Great Horklesey – 128
Great Waltham – 45
Grey (Lady Jane) –124
Grey (Lady Katharine) – 124
Grey (Lord) – 128, 129
Griffin (Sir John) – 93
Gunner's Creek – 75
Gurdon-Rebow (Mr.) – 78, 81

Hadleigh – 78, 118
Hadrian – 120
Hamford Water – 39
Hallingbury – 78, 113
Halstead – 114
Harlow – 91, 111
Harlowbury – 91, 92
Harlow Mill – 91, 115
Hainack (Syd) – 99
Harris (Frank) – 77, 81
Harwick – 38, 39, *71*
Hastings the Dane – 97
Hatfield Forest – 80
Haverhill – 113
Helmingham Hall – 125
Hempstead – 77
Henham – 77
Henry VIII – 45
Hereward the Wake – 86
Herongate – 83, 87, 119
Heron Hall – 119
Heron Lodge – 61, 69, 73
Hexham – 123
Heybridge – 10
Heydon – 95
High Easter – 113
Hoare (Benjamin) – 45

130

Holehaven Creek – 119
Hone (Nathaniel) – 100
Hone (Mrs.) – 101
Honywood (Mrs.) – 81
Horeham – 77, 78
Hornchurch – 84
Houblon (Archer) – 78, 80
House of Lords – 124
Howard (Thomas) – 93

Ingatestone Hall – 124
Infanta of Spain – 127
Ipswich – 47
Ironside (Edmund) – 16, 17

James I – 93, 125, 126, 127
Jockey Club – 55

Kelvedon – 59, *59*, 60, *63*
Kersey – 114
Key (Dennis) – 107
Kings Hill – 105
Knight (Sir John) – 129
Knights (Edward) – 12
Knowles (Robert) – 30

Laindon Hill – 84
Lamidel – 69
Langenhoe – 73
Langham – 55
Langleys Park – 81
Latchingdon – 10, 11, 12
Lavenham – 114
Lawless Court – 104
Leavett (Will) – 35, 70, 75
Leigh Marsh – 65
Lewin (Thomas) – 28
Lillingstone Lovell (Bucks.) – 122, 125
Linnett (Walter) – 30, 33
Lisle (Sir George) – 50
Little Horklesley – 128
Little Waltham – 45
London – 47, 59, 77, 84, 89, 91, 110, 111, 112, 117, 125
Lobster Smack – 118, 119
Lucas (Sir Charles) – 50
Lympne (Kent) – 27, 28

Magdalen Laver – 113
Magna Carta – 106
Magrini (Prof.) – 70
Maldon – 6, 7, 9, 10, 12, *13*, 15, 73, 83, 84, 114, 128
Maltravers (Lady) – 125
Manningtree – *56*, 114
Mansion House – 91
Maplin Sands – 70
Mary Queen of Scots – 70
Masefield (John) – 55
Maynards – 77, 78
McMullen (Alex B.) – 61
Mersea – 7, 51, 73, 75, 96, 97, 98, *98*, 99, 101, 107
Mildmay – 78, 104, 106
Mill Creek – 62
Millington (Sir Thomas) – 129
Montagu (Lord) – 106

Morton (Earl of) – 70
Mountnessing – 128
Moynes – 77
Munnings (Sir Alfred) – 53, 54
Murrell (Cunning) – 118
Mussett (Douglas) – 101

Napoleon II – 70
Nettlestead – 122, 123, 125
Neville (Hon. Robin) – 95
New Hall – 45
Newmarket – 53, 55
Norden – 77, 78
Norfolk – 25, 47, 57, 65, 67
North Sea – 70, 74
Northey Island – 7, *10*, 13
Norsey Wood – 84
Norwich – 47, 48
Nugent (Earl) – 129

Old Hall – 98
Ongar – 54, 113
Orford Ness – 70
Othona – 7, 25, 28, 97
Overbury (Sir Thomas) – 126
Oxbird – 65, 67
Oysters – 47, 107

Paglesham – *102, 104,* 107, 109
Parker (C.W.) – 29
Parker (Oxley) – 28
Paxman (James N.) – 62
Perigord – 69
Petre (Lord) – 78, 80, 83, 84, 85, 86, 124
Pevensey – 25, 27, 28
Pevsner – 90
Picketts Bushes – 120
Pinkie – 123
Plume (Dr.) – 7
Portchester – 25, 27
Portsmouth – 25
Porters – 77
Potton Island – 20, 21, 39
Ptolemy (Claudius) – 120

Quendon Park – 81

Rainham – 84
Rayleigh – 78
Ray Island – 97, 98
Rays'n Channel – 106
Reculver (Kent) – 27
Richborough (Kent) – 27, 28
Roach river – 107
Rochford – 68, 78, 104, *106*
Roman – 2
 – forts, 25, 30, 47, 49, 97, 107, 117
Romford – 84
Roothings – 89, 113, 114, 115
Roper (Anne) – 19
Rothenstein (Sir John) – 54
Roswell – 45
Russell (Jesse) – 84
Rutton (Leslie) – 127

Saffron Walden – 89, *92, 94,* 113
St. Botolph Priory – *49,* 49, 50
St. Osyth – 38
Salter (Dr. J. H.) – 61

Saxon – 7, 13, 14, 25, 29, 51, 86, 91, 120
Saxton – 78
Shellow Bowels – 114
Sheppey – 15
Shirley (Evelyn) – 77, 79, 80
Shoeburyness – 15, 65
Sible Hedingham – 77
Sichel (Walter) – 55
South (Bob) – 101
Southend – 15, 65, 83, *117,* 128
South Essex – 84
South Ockendon – 84
Spence (Sir Basil) – 112
Stamp (Charlie) – 118, 121
Stansted – 111
Stevens (Jack) – 84
Stifford – 84
Stoke-by-Nayland – 53
Stort – 92
Stour (river) – 54, *56, 57*
Stratford-on-Avon – 77
Stratford St. Mary – 53
Streona (Edric) – 17
Strood – 51, 97

Thames – 15, 84, 91, 120
Thaxted – 78, 113
Thomas (Bert) – 99
Thorndon – 78, 80, *82,* 84, 85, 87, *87*
Thorpe Bay – 65
Thurrock – 117
Thurslet Creek – 62
Tilbury – 65, 121
Tillingham – 66
Tiptree – 61, 63
Tollesbury – 61, 62, 63, 65, 69, 71, 73, *74*
Tolleshunt D'Arcy – 62
Tower (Christopher) – 80
Tufnell (J. J.) – 81
Tufnell (Mr.) – 78
Tufnell (Samuel) – 45
Tyrell (Sir John) – 119

Ulster – 126

Van Cropenbrough – 22, 120

Waldon Abbey – 93
Wallasea – 10, 11, 103, 107
Walsingham (Elizabeth) – 125
Walton (Suffolk) – 27
Washington (Rev. Lawrence) – 7
War of the Roses – 123
Warwick (Countess of) – 80
Whitaker (John) – 80
Weald Hall – 78, 80
Webster (Capt. Charles) – 91
Went (Jimmy) – 119
Wentworths – 122, 123, 125, 127, 128, 129
Wentworth (Baroness) – 122
Wentworth (Manors) – 123
Wentworth (Paul) – 122
Wentworth (Peter) – 125
Wentworth (Philip) – 123
Wentworth (Sir John) – 123, 124, 125, 126, 127, 129

Wentworth (Thomas) – 123, 124
Wentworth Woodhouse – 83, 92
West Indies – 128
Wethersfield – 128
Wick Marshes – 73
Wildfowlers Association – 70

Willett (John) – 31
Wilkin (Arthur) – 61
William the Conqueror – 48
Windsor – 122
Winchelsea – 128
Witham – 113

Wivenhoe – 51, 78, 81
Woodford – 115
Writtle – 113
Wyatt ('Adm.' Bill) – 100

Yarmouth – 59